HISTORY OF BASEBALL

Days of the Rosewood Bat and the Silver Ball

Richard J. Staats

HERITAGE BOOKS
2004

HERITAGE BOOKS
AN IMPRINT OF HERITAGE BOOKS, INC.

Books, CDs, and more – Worldwide

For our listing of thousands of titles see our website at
www.HeritageBooks.com

Published 2004 by
HERITAGE BOOKS, INC.
Publishing Division
65 E. Main St.
Westminster, Maryland 21157

COPYRIGHT © 2003 RICHARD J. STAATS

OTHER HERITAGE BOOKS BY THE AUTHOR:

A Grassroots History of the American Civil War, Volume I:
The Life and Times of Pvt. Ephraim Cooper, One of Mr. Lincoln's First Volunteers

A Grassroots History of the American Civil War, Volume II:
The Bully Seventh, Ohio Volunteer Infantry

A Grassroots History of the American Civil War, Volume III: Captain Cotter's Battery

A Grassroots History of the American Civil War, Volume IV:
The Life and Times of Colonel William Stedman of the 6th Ohio Cavalry

All rights reserved. No part of this book may be reproduced or transmitted in any form or by any means, electronic or mechanical, including photocopying, recording or by any information storage and retrieval system without written permission from the author, except for the inclusion of brief quotations in a review.

International Standard Book Number: 0-7884-2466-1

TABLE OF CONTENTS

Introduction v

Chapter One – Reborn on the 4th of July 1

Chapter Two – Of War And Base Ball 6

Chapter Three – The Spirit of the Game 29

Chapter Four – The Feud 41

Chapter Five – The Rosewood Bat and the Silver Ball 61

Chapter Six – Up And At 'Em Again ! 81

Chapter Seven – Where Have All The Trophies Gone? 95

Chapter Eight – An Epitaph For The Star Club 109

Chapter Nine – The Legacy 127

Footnotes 137

Bibliography 143

Team Index 145

Players Index 147

General Index 151

INTRODUCTION

This book is the result of the author's being a Civil War buff and a lifetime Cleveland Indians' fan. I vaguely remember when the Tribe triumphed over the Boston Braves in the 1948 World Series. Folks huddled around the wooden cabinet radios of that day, hanging on every word of the broadcast, and cheering a good play as if they were at the ballpark. However, I vividly recall that bright sunny afternoon in the summer of 1954 when I and a host of other youthful players of the Greater Akron Baseball Federation packed the left field bleachers at the old Municipal Stadium. The atmosphere seemed to be electrified as the Tribe charged onto the field. At third base was my favorite player, Al Rosen. In spite of a broken nose and a fractured finger, Rosen played through the pain. He still contributed a .300 batting average and 24 home runs to the Tribe's offense that year. Rosen and I both wore number 7. At second base was Bobby Avila, who was on his way to leading the American League in batting average with an impressive .341 average. Early Wynn was on the mound that day, and the aggressive and highly competitive right hander hurled the home team to a 4-3 victory. All was well with the world.

Then came the 1954 World Series. Cleveland had set a record with 111 wins against only 43 losses (.721). We sat and fidgeted beside the radio, hanging on every utterance of Jimmy Dudley's friendly southern drawl. When the Tribe lost four straight games to the New York Giants, disappointment bordering on depression hovered over us for days, some of which lasts to this very day.

However, 1954 was not a total loss by any means. The Cleveland Browns won the Eastern Division of the National Football League with a 9-3 record; and the team went on to thump the Detroit Lions 56-10 in the championship game. The Ohio State Buckeyes also added to the glory by beating USC 20-7 in the Rose Bowl and

The Manchester Boys of 1954

Press.

[*The Manchester Boys of 1954 – Kneeling, Roger Silknitter, Tom Lambert, Jeff King, Jim Carmany. Standing, Phil Sitts, Jim Ling, Richard Staats, Dave Queen, Tom Lent, Richard Kurlich, Roger Davis, Coach Joe Slayman.*

Thanks to Coach Slayman, "Joe" to his players, the team sported new uniforms. Joe and Ruby, his wife, went to the local merchants for financial support; thus, this team of "country kids" came into existence and was the only team in the school district that summer.

Long before the term "role model" came into sports jargon, Joe was the epitome of one. The ex-Marine had been an excellent high school athlete, who could punt and pass a football with the best. Joe did not smoke, drink, or swear; and although he may have been tempted, he never berated or belittled a player. If Coach Slayman had a flaw, it was his penchant for very unfunny jokes.

The young lads gazing into the camera on this bright sunny summer day may have been unaware of it, but they were the luckiest kids on the face of the earth.]

The passions of being a Civil War buff and a baseball fan collided as I was researching some of the local Civil War veterans. Microfilm of the newspapers in Portage, Summit, Cuyahoga, and Trumbull Counties provided a gold mine of excellent material. In tracing the postwar activities of some veterans, I discovered that some of them were "Base Ball" players. (Baseball was not a compound word in those days.) Like my magical year of 1954, the year of 1867 seemed to be the magical year of that era when Base Ball enthusiasm exploded across northeast Ohio. Base Ball Clubs sprung up in every city, small town, and hamlet. Challenges to "matches" flew through the area.

Perhaps a Base Ball match in the Civil War days was a form of escapism. Few, if any, veterans went home to live happily ever after. Bitterness over reconstruction politics made for an uncertain future. Nevertheless, Base Ball seemed to bring out the best in America. Bravery, good sportsmanship, self-discipline, and striving to do one's best were intrinsic values of the game.

It was a time when the "ladies" in their horse-drawn carriages, dapper gentlemen, and frisky boys crowded up to the foul lines to get a closer look at the action. Oftentimes, the spectators became part of the action due to their close proximity to the playing area and in their efforts to peer around the person in front of them. In those days Base Ball was considered to be a "gentleman's" game, and the gentlemen played under a set of rules found in a small booklet titled *Beadle's Dime Base Ball Player*. It was truly a sportsman's game in which the umpire was treated with the utmost respect.

Yet, Base Ball in the 1860's was a rugged, manly endeavor. No man would dare to wear a glove to catch a rocketing hard-rubber ball; only sissies would stoop to such behavior! In addition, the wearing of equipment of any kind might impugn one's character and cause the spectators to question the player's courage. The cup and the jockstrap, as we know them today, did not exist in the 1860's. Thus, the unsightly crotch-grabbing of the modern day players was not in evidence in the post-Civil War years; after all, it was a gentleman's game – although it could be quite painful at times. Another challenge to the post-war Base Ball Clubs was the lack of groomed playing surfaces. Their unmanicured Elysian fields might require a fielder to negotiate a large tree while chasing a fly ball, to avoid angry yellow jackets swarming out of the ground in the outfield, or to dodge "cow piles" and "road apples" while chasing the bounding sphere. This was no kid's game.

Originally, the main theme of this research was the quest of the Ravenna Star Base Ball Club to win its own trophy, "the Rosewood Bat and the Silver Ball," at the Portage County Fair in 1867. In order to present a better picture of the Base Ball atmosphere in which the Star Club played, as well as satisfying historical inquisitiveness, other areas of Base Ball interest have been included in the text. For example, how and when did the game enter into northeast Ohio? What were the rules in Beadle's booklet? What did the players on the Star Club do for a living, and what became of them in later life? Just how good was the Star Club in relation to other teams in the area?

For the author, it was a joy to read the old newspaper articles. They are presented in their original form so that you may also enjoy the unique spirit of the National Pastime in its infancy. The players and their fans probably submitted the game reports to the editors. However, the *Portage County Democrat*'s editor appeared to be quite interested in Base Ball, and he may have reported his own observations. The Base Ball reports are more than statistics. They preserved the aura, the excitement, the high value of sportsmanship, the humor, and the community pride that accompanied our National Pastime in the mid-1800's.

    I am deeply grateful for the cheerful and competent assistance provided by Marie Karas Herlevi, Mike Eliot, and the staff at the Akron-Summit County Library, the Cleveland Public Library, Carol Willsey Bell and the Trumbull County Library in Warren, Cindy Gaynor and the Reed Library in Ravenna, Gwen Mayer of the Hudson Library Archives, and Lisa Johnson of the Hiram College Archives. A special thanks goes to Charles Maimone, the caretaker of Maple Grove Cemetery in Ravenna. Mr. Maimone, a former youth baseball coach and umpire, provided many good leads toward finding information about the Base Ball players and Civil War veterans. Richard A. Gardner, author of *History of an Ohio Community, Manchester*, generously gave his time and assistance, which was essential to the last chapter. It was a pleasant trip down memory lane to visit Ike Williams in his barbershop in Manchester. Ike was an outstanding baseball player in his youth, and he has a keen memory for baseball and other interesting stories. Mark Heppner, Vice President and Curator – Museum Service Division, Stan Hywet Hall and Gardens in Akron, provided the pictures of the Vintage Base Ball players in action. Mark and his fellow Base Ballers keep the true spirit of sportsmanship and competition alive for the National Pastime. The concept for this book would never have gotten off the ground if it were not for Coach Joe Slayman, who made baseball so much fun back in the 50's.

This book is dedicated to all of the kids, young and old, who just loved to play the game of baseball.

Richard J. Staats

CHAPTER ONE

Reborn On The 4ᵀᴴ Of July

The old historian stared at the writing paper on his desk, which was bathed in the warm glow of the oil lamp. A smile began to ease the wrinkles on his weather worn face as he fondly remembered his departed parents, the old homestead, and the exhilaration of his youth. He was born during the presidency of Andrew Jackson. "Old Hickory may have been 64 years old, however he and the young United States of America were a vigorous lot back then.

It was a time when Independence Day was *the* grandest day of the whole year. The old historian recalled the excited anticipation as July 4th approached back in those halcyon days, and he jotted his remembrances on his paper.

> ... Independence Day, as the Fourth of July was called, was universally observed. A strong effort was made to finish hoeing corn before that anniversary. A large amount of gunpowder was burned (it was before the day of fire-crackers and torpedoes), commencing early in the morning and lasting until the supply gave out...[1]

Indeed, in those days Independence Day was ushered in at midnight as gunpowder continually exploded in disregard of the many city ordinances against explosives. Between twelve and one o'clock in the morning, a gun squad fired a national salute into the black sky. Then followed the clangor of bells, martial music, and a torch light parade through the streets. The noisy excitement continued through the night.

At dawn's first light, the cannon blasted another thundering salute. Gradually, the streets became thronged with gaily-clad children, parents dressed in their Sunday best, and an occasional frisky yapping dog. Horse-and-buggy traffic clogged the main streets. The national banner and beautiful red, white and blue bunting adorned every business and residential edifice. As the excited sea of humanity streamed toward the local park, the citizens from all around the area hallooed to friends, relatives, and neighbors.

The buzzing crowd at the park was motioned to silence. Out of respect for the occasion, men and boys arose and removed their hats. The Declaration of Independence was read at the beginning of the exercises. Then the orations, spoken in English and German, were received with loud patriotic approvals. At intervals, the martial band and the gun squad threw in "enlivening notes." [2]

During the day, the patriots and veterans of the War of 1812 gathered at the courthouse. The *Portage Sentinel* noted that the "little band of PATRIOTS, now numbering three score, with silver locks and feeble limbs, tottering upon their staves, came up on Freedom's natal day to greet each other ere they follow their brave companions who have gone before...Scarce a veteran cheek was dry when "Hail Columbia" and "Yankee Doodle" were enthusiastically rendered by the band, the Soldiers standing with heads uncovered as a tribute to the National airs." [3]

Amidst the enthusiasm of the patriotic speeches, the blaring brass instruments of the martial bands, exploding gunpowder, refreshments of cakes, cheese, and whiskey (the latter only if you were old enough and not a "temperance man"), what could be more fitting and American than a game of BASEBALL !

"Dr. Oliver Wendell Holmes ... said to the reporter of a Boston paper that base-ball was one of the sports of his college days at Harvard, and Dr. Holmes graduated in 1829." [4] From this revelation it is quite likely that some enterprising Yankee sportsman/pioneer brought some form of the game of baseball from New England to the Connecticut Western Reserve of northeast Ohio prior to that time.

Walter Johnson Dickinson, the "old historian," who was born in Randolph, Portage County, Ohio, obviously recalled with pleasure that terrific July 4th of his youth when the boys scurried into a field to play that wonderful game.

> ...On one occasion in the early settlement, for some unexplained or forgotten cause, the youngsters had two days for the holiday [July 4th] and played ball so hard and long that they could with difficulty work for some days after... [5]

Walter and his fellow enthusiasts for "playing ball" then passed the love of the game to their sons, grandsons, and younger neighbors.

By the mid-1840's, the spirit of Manifest Destiny was sweeping over the youthful United States with an apostolic zeal. For many Americans the doctrine of Manifest Destiny meant that the spread of American institutions was designed and ordained by a higher being. The western expansion was a prime example. Whether or not an individual was capable of verbalizing it, certainly an unlimited faith in success, a positive attitude, and American pride were required for a man to load his family and meager possessions into an ox cart. Then they braved the weather and physical hazards in their trek over the Appalachian Mountains and beyond. The same spirit pervaded Base Ball; in fact, the game had its own manifest destiny.

In August 1846, the 27-year old master wordsmith and editor of the *Brooklyn Daily Eagle* penned an editorial, "Brooklyn Young Men – Athletic Exercises," in which he exhibited his lifelong love affair with Base Ball.

> In our sun-down perambulations, of late, through the outer parts of Brooklyn, we have observed several parties of youngsters playing "base," a certain game of ball. We wish such sights were more common among us. In the practice of athletic and manly sports the young men of nearly all American cities are very deficient – perhaps more so than any other country that could be mentioned ... Let us go forth awhile, and get better air in our lungs. Let us leave our close rooms ... the game of ball is glorious. [6]
>
> Walt Whitman

Forty-two years later, Whitman still possessed "base-ball's" spirit of manifest destiny when he wrote to his friend Horace Traubel

> I like your interest in sports – ball, chiefest of all – base-ball particularly: base-ball is our game: the American game: I connect it with our national character. Sports take people out of doors, get them filled with oxygen – generate some of the brutal customs (so-called brutal customs) which, after all, tend to habituate people to a necessary physical stoicism. We are some ways a dyspeptic, nervous set: anything which will repair such losses may be regarded as a blessing to the race. [7]

When Trauble referred to baseball as "the hurrah game of the republic," Whitman spiritedly responded:

> That's beautiful: the hurrah game! Well – it's our game: that's the chief fact in connection with it: America's game: has the snap, go, fling, of the American atmosphere – belongs as much to our institutions, fits into them as significantly, as our constitutions, laws: is just as important in the sum total of our historical life. [8]

Whitman's rhapsody on baseball was genuine, and it is well documented. However, history has shown that this wonderful pastime quickly lent itself to mythology, conjecture, and plain old wishful thinking. As in all the ages, there have been saints and sinners, believers and scoffers. Of course, it is a free country and one can believe anything that he chooses: a) Gen. Abner Doubleday, of Civil War fame, invented baseball b) the forbidden fruit that Eve gave to Adam was a big red apple c) Paul Bunyon and Babe, his big blue ox, created the lakes in Minnesota d) Babe Ruth called his home run shot for a kid e) none of the above.

There even were rumors that an Illinois rail splitter not only wielded a wicked ax, but also swung a mean Base Ball bat. Some say that this giant plainsman, known as Abe, became a well-known lawyer who dodged important legal matters in court just to play Base Ball with the local Springfield, Illinois boys. It was said that in his later life Abe would take his little son, Tad, by his tiny hand, and they would sit with the plebians along the foul line of some Base Ball field in Washington, DC.

Yet, Judge Charles S. Zane, a contemporary of the rail splitter, stated that Abraham Lincoln played handball, not Base Ball. Since the judge was a member of the United States Supreme Court, the veracity of the account has merit.

> Lincoln played ball pretty much all the day before his nomination, played at what is called fives [handball], knocking a ball up against a wall that served as an alley. He loved this game, his only physical game that I knew of. Lincoln said: "This game makes my shoulders feel well." [9]

One would think that if Lincoln had been an ardent Base Ball player and enthusiastic fan of the game, a multitude of scribes would have written hefty tomes on the subject. Paraphrasing the work of the great hurler, Gaylord Perry, who was known to apply moisture to the ball, at least one book would have been titled, *Me and the Splitter*.

Nevertheless, as 1860 rolled around, Lincoln's attention was riveted to politics, not Base Ball. But the "boys of summer" concentrated on Base Ball, not politics.

CHAPTER TWO

OF WAR AND BASE BALL

The ominous threat of civil war hovered over the land on April 10, 1861. The editor of the *Portage County Democrat* anxiously informed his readers: "War At The Door. At our going to press the news by yesterday's mails was of the most decisive character, and if reliable, before another issue of our paper, actual hostilities will have commenced, probably at Charleston." However, some of the young men were turning their fancy to other pursuits that spring. In the same issue, the *Democrat* published the following local news article.

BASE BALL --- The young men of Ravenna have organized a base ball club, and are cultivating that exhilarating and pleasing game with great vigor. A few afternoons of practice have rendered quite a number of them "experts." The games are conducted by two captains, an umpire, and secretary, who are governed by rules laid down in Beadle's Dime Base Ball Player for 1861. The grounds used for the meetings of the club are the commons upon Main street of the C.& P. R.R. depot, where upon a bright afternoon large crowds of spectators gather to witness the sport.[10]

The rule book, which the Ravenna club followed, was a thin 3 ½ by 5 ½ inch booklet that could be purchased at the Ravenna Book Store at that time. The cost, of course, was one thin dime.[11] A perusal of this book provides a description of the game of Base-Ball in 1861.

Before examining the rules, one should consider the reasons for having the rules. Some of the reasons that readily come to mind are fairness, safety, standardization of the game and equipment, and *hopefully* to render a smooth conduct of the game with a minimum of arguing. Next, one should try to imagine what condition existed that prompted the formation of a particular rule. For example, in Section 14 of the *Dime Base-Ball Player*, the rule defines the runner being thrown out at first base. Some previous variations of the game permitted the fielder to throw the ball at the runner for an out. Imagine the runner streaking to a base and the fielder whistling a throw into the runner's body or pegging one off the runner's head. Another example is Section 21, which states that the runner is safe if obstructed by a fielder. Prior to this rule, one can imagine a second baseman coyly positioning himself so that the runner would have to go around him; or at worst, a nasty second baseman sneakily tripping or physically wiping out the runner while the outfielders are chasing his base hit.

Before listing the rules in Beadle's edition, Henry Chadwick waxed eloquently about the attributes of a base-ball player in 1861; and certainly when the young Ravenna players read this, their chests stuck out even further with pride.

> ... Base Ball to be played thoroughly, requires the possession of muscular strength, great agility, quickness of eye, readiness of hand, and many other faculties of mind and body that mark the man of nerve. [12]

The first convention of Base-Ball Players was held in New York City in May, 1857. Its purpose was to establish a permanent code of rules. At the next convention in March of 1858, the National Association of Base-Ball Players came into being. Here are their rules for 1861. [13]

Section 1 – The ball. It should be 5 ½ to 5 ¾ ounces avoirdupois ; 9 ½ to 9 ¾ in circumference. It was composed of "india-rubber" and yarn, and it was covered with leather. The ball was furnished by the challenging club, and it became the property of the winning club as a "trophy of victory."

Section 2 – The bat. The bat must be round and no thicker than 2 ½ inches in diameter in the thickest part. It had to be made of wood. It could be any length to suit the "striker."

Section 3 – The bases – There must be four bases securely fastened to the ground. The bases were to be set 30 yards apart and in a square. The base was to measure one square foot. It was to be a canvas bag filled with sand or sawdust. Home base and the "pitcher's point" were to be marked by a flat circular iron plate that was painted or enameled white.

Section 4 – This rule defined the order of the bases ---1st, 2nd, etc. It also established a chalk line from home to first and from home to third.

Section 5 – The pitcher's line was four yards in length, centered on a line from home to second base. The pitcher must deliver the ball as near as possible over the home base. [Note: There were no bases on balls.] He had no right to pitch to the catcher especially. This section admonished the umpire to enforce the rule. [The pitcher delivered the ball under-handed. The above-the-belt motion was not allowed until 1884.[14]]

Section 6 – "The ball must be pitched, not jerked or thrown to the bat; and whenever the pitcher draws back his hand, or moves with the apparent purpose or pretension to deliver the ball, he shall so deliver, and he must have neither foot in advance of the line at the time of delivering the ball; and if he fails in either of these particulars, then it shall be declared a baulk."

Section 7 – When a baulk is made by the pitcher, every player running the bases is entitled to one base without being put out.

Section 8 – This defined a foul ball. If the ball hit first in fair territory in front of the bases, it was ruled a fair ball. Anything that hit off the side of a building, fence, or tree was to be covered by ground rules before the game commenced.

Section 9 – " 1 run" was counted when a player crossed home base.

Section 10 – The batter could run on a missed third strike.

Section 11 – The striker is out if a foul ball is caught on the fly or first bounce.

Section 12 – If the last strike was caught in the air or first bounce, the batter was out.

Section 13 – A fly ball catch or a ball caught on the first bounce resulted in an out.

Section 14 – If the ball was "held by an adversary on the first base, before the striker touches that base," he was out.

Section 15 – A player touched by the ball "while in play in the hands of an adversary, without some part of his person being on a base," he was out.

Section 16 – No ace [a run] nor base can be made upon a foul ball, nor when a ball is caught on the fly. Runners must return to the

Carman "Four Fingers" Lubrano, the "hurler" for the Black Sox, assumes a classic pose and then properly delivers the "hurl" according to Beadle's rule book. "Lil Joe" Turner, the "striker," awaits a good "hurl."

bases and may be put out "in the same manner as the striker when running to first base."

Section 17 – This rule established the batting order. It also required the striker to stand within three feet on either side of home base on a line through the base and parallel with that of the pitcher.

Section 18 – The striker was required to keep one foot on the line mentioned in the previous section.

Section 19 – This established the requirement of running in the base line. If the runner was three feet out of it to avoid a tag, he was ruled out.

Section 20 – Interfering with a fielder resulted in the runner being called out.

Section 21 – Obstruction of a runner by a fielder resulted in the runner being declared safe. In case of a conflict between sections 20 and 21, "The umpire must alone decide this difficult question, and he should never hesitate to put a stop to any tendency to infringe the rules in this respect."

Section 22 – "If a player stops the ball with his hat or cap, or take it from the hands of a party not engaged in the game, no player can be put out unless the ball shall have been settled in the hands of the pitcher.... It would be as well for the umpire to warn the spectators, previous to the commencement of the game, of the fact that any stoppage of the ball, such as referred to in the above rule, will act equally against both parties, and request them to let the ball pass in every case."

Section 23 – Other than the above rule, the striker is out on a caught fly ball or one bounce.

Section 24 – Runners cannot score if the striker is the third out.

Section 25 – When the "third hand" is put out, an "innings" must be concluded. [One earlier variation of the game allowed all of the team to bat in their half of an inning.]

Section 26 – This rule established a 9 inning game with extra innings in case of a tie.

Section 27 – There must be nine players per side. They had to be regular members for at least 30 days and not have played for another club during that time. After the game commenced, there were no substitutions or changes in the lineup unless for reasons of illness or injury.

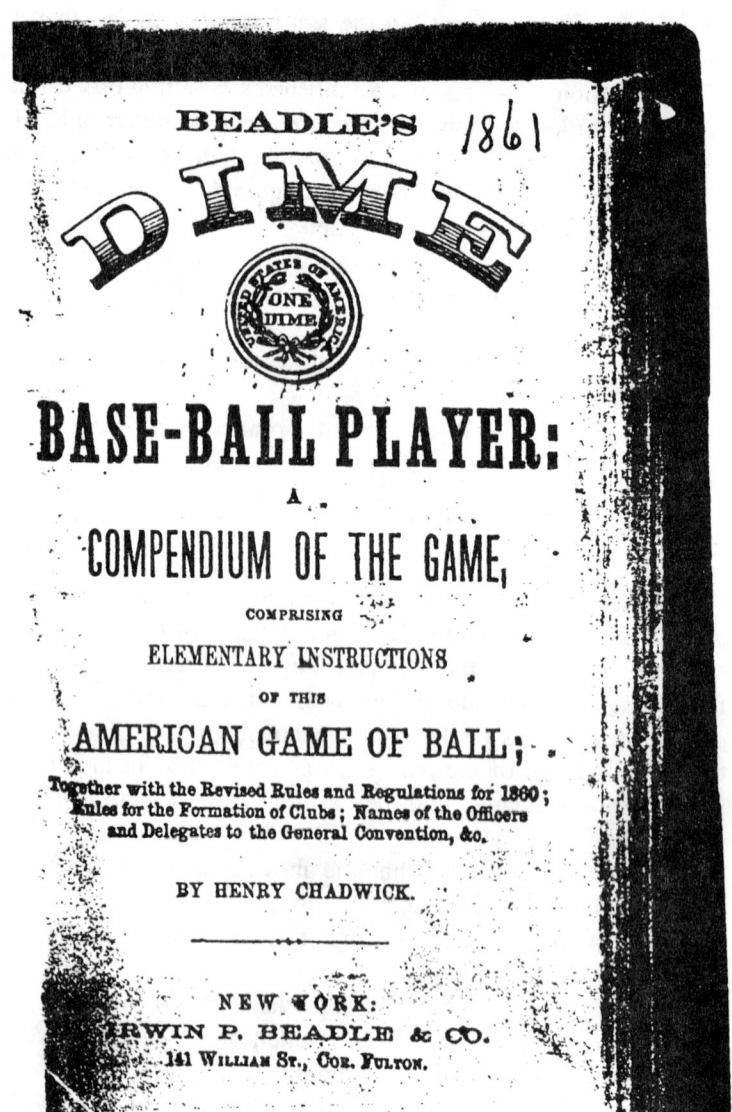

Courtesy of the Cleveland Public Library

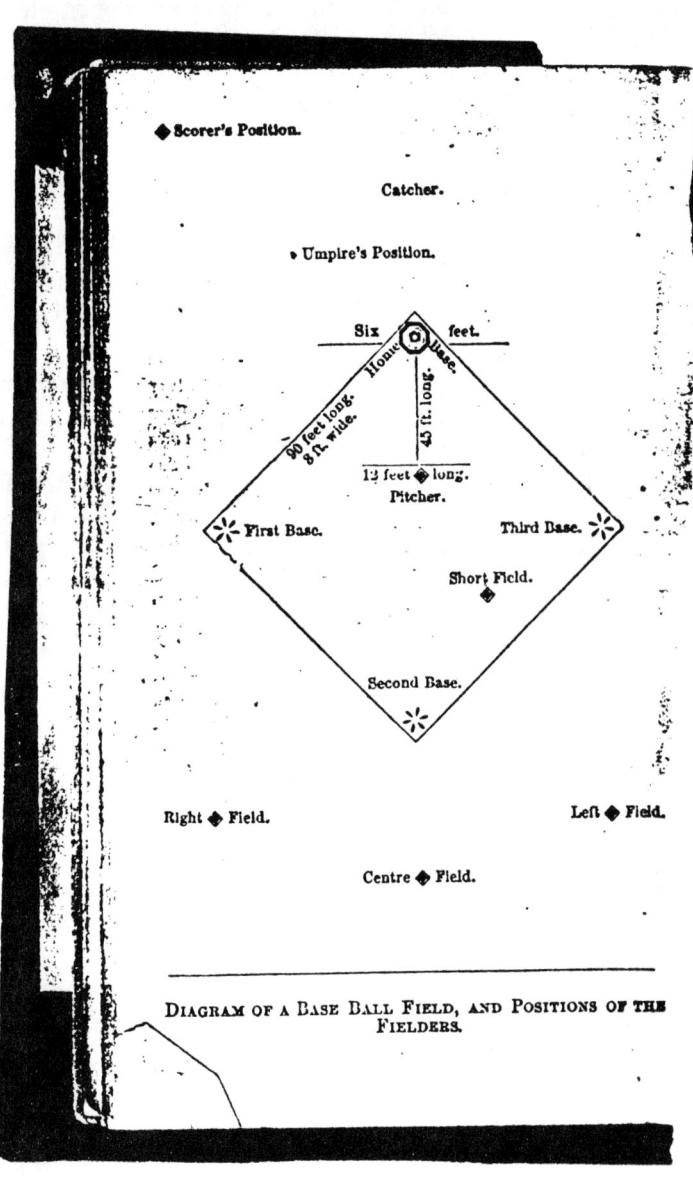

DIAGRAM OF A BASE BALL FIELD, AND POSITIONS OF THE FIELDERS.

Courtesy of the Cleveland Public Library

Section 28 – This rule concerned the umpire's duties. He had to make sure that the equipment and field markings were regulated. Then he was to keep a record of the game, judge fair and unfair play, determine all disputes, and give especial attention in declaring all foul balls and baulks in a distinct and audible manner.

Section 29 – The umpire was to be selected by the team captains. Each club appointed a scorer.

Section 30 – This rule stressed "NO BETTING" by a player, umpire, or scorer either directly or indirectly. [Betting on games severely threatened the integrity of the game even in 1861. Later in the booklet, Chadwick again stressed the threat of gambling to the game of baseball. He felt that gambling caused fan interference as well as taking away the interest and excitement of the game.] This section also authorized the umpire to "dismiss any transgressor."

Section 31 – The umpire was authorized to suspend play. Five innings made an official game, and a shortened game was decided by the last even innings.

Section 32 – Special ground rules were to be established by the home team and announced to the opponents prior to the game.

Section 33 – – Fans were not permitted to approach or speak to the participants during the contest "unless by special request of the umpire."

Section 34 – Umpires and scorers must be members of a "Base Ball Club governed by these rules."

Section 35 – Teams must appear on time. If either party was 15 minutes late, "...the party so failing shall admit a defeat."

Section 36 – No person in arrears to any other club or who receives "compensation for his services as a player, shall be competent to play in any match."

Section 37 – If a striker repeatedly does not swing at good pitches, the umpire must issue a warning and thereafter call strikes. Chadwick thought that this behavior on the part of the batter was particularly annoying.

Section 38 – "Every match hereafter made shall be decided by a single game, unless otherwise mutually agreed upon by the contesting teams." [15]

The little booklet then gave pointers on how to play the positions and to give information on "Junior" clubs, players who were 14-20 years of age.

Chadwick also credited Alexander Joy Cartwright of the New York Knickerbocker Base Ball Club for these current rules. Cartwright wanted the game to be less of a contact sport and more of a gentleman's game, so he and his Knickerbockers devised 14 rules, which were first used on June 19, 1846 at Hoboken, New Jersey.[16]

So, after familiarizing themselves with the rules and playing tips in the booklet published by Irwin P. Beadle & Co., the young men of the Ravenna Star Base Ball Club were ready to play and enjoy this wonderful "gentleman's game."

Then, two days after the *Democrat*'s announcement of the organization of the Ravenna Star Base Ball Club, the idyllic, carefree days of Base Ball on the commons began to dwindle. On April 12, 1861 at 4:30 A.M., Fort Sumter was fired upon. However, the prevailing thought was that the War of the Rebellion would be about a three-months affair or last until one large battle decided the issue. Some of the "boys" continued to play Base Ball during the summer; and the *Portage County Democrat*, August 21, 1861, reported: "The Ravenna Base Ball Club have regular meetings every pleasant 'sunset' on the green, west of the railroad depot. The games are quite interesting, and many of the players are becoming experts."[17] Thereafter, the *Democrat* ceased to report any Base Ball activity. Whether the editor thought it inappropriate to print such frolicsome news during the national crisis or if the Ravenna Club temporarily disbanded is unknown. In the next four years some of the players would leave for war on the C & P Railroad tracks located adjacent to their baseball field. At least four members of the 1867 edition of the Star Base Ball Club would serve in the military.

George M. Phillips entered the 128th Ohio Volunteer Infantry on November 23, 1863 for three years. George was mustered in at the age of 19, and he became a lieutenant. The 128th was principally engaged in guarding the Confederate officers who were held as prisoners on Johnson's Island in Sandusky Bay of Lake Erie. The regiment frequently furnished detachments for elsewhere. George mustered out of the service with Company D on July 13, 1865.[18]

Morton H. Phillips, George's younger brother, entered the war at its end, and thus he was spared a lot of hardship. At the age of 18 Morton entered the 39th Ohio Infantry on April 6, 1865 for one year. Someone who was drafted paid for a substitute to take his place; and Morton was that substitute. On March 19-21 the 39th was at Bentonville, North Carolina. Morton mustered out with his company on July 9, 1865.

George E. King served in the 14th Battalion of the Ohio National Guard. When his unit was called to serve for 100 days, King was mustered into Company G of the 171st Ohio Regiment. At Keller's Bridge, Kentucky the 171st was mauled by Gen. John Hunt Morgan's rebel cavalry, which resulted in 13 killed and 54 wounded for the Ohio regiment. The 19-year old sergeant completed his 100-day stint by guarding prisoners at Johnson's Island. [19]

John Henry Oakley was 19 years old when the war broke out, and he immediately enlisted as a volunteer in the three-month's service with the 7th Ohio Infantry. In October of 1861, John re-enlisted for three years in Battery I, 1st Ohio Volunteer Light Artillery, and he served until December 12, 1864. John saw some hard campaigning. He was at Bull Run, fought in the Shenandoah Valley against Stonewall Jackson's men, Chancellorsville, Gettysburg, Mission Ridge at Chattanooga, and all of the Atlanta Campaign under Gen. Sherman. [20]

The Civil War may have put a crimp into the hopes and plans of local baseball teams, but the war undoubtedly spread the popularity of the game. At Washington, D. C., the hub of the Union Army in the east, many soldiers probably witnessed the "Base Ball match game" between the "Nationals" and the "Washingtons" in June of 1862. The Nationals won by a score of 62-22. The *Washington Star* reported the game.

> On the part of the Nationals, Ned Hibbs' batting was superb, he making five homeruns. While Walden took care of all balls which came in his region, and made several very fine catches.
> On the part of the Washingtons, Messrs. Sharretts and Marr, as catcher and pitcher, were also excellent. Johnson the first and McIntire on the second bases, played well. Potter, as short, was very active, and with McHeren did some fine fielding. [21]

On Christmas Day of 1862, over 40,000 Union soldiers watched a game between teams selected from the 165th New York Volunteer Infantry, Duryea's Zouaves. [22]

In Wiley's *The Life of Billy Yank*, "A Vermont soldier gave this description: The ball was soft, and a great bounder. To put a base runner out, he had to be hit by the ball, thrown by the pitcher... A game between the Eighth and 114th Vermont Regiments near Franklin, Louisiana, in February of 1864 was won by the former 21-9. The "first team" of the Ninth New York Regiment beat the Fifty-first New Yorkers 31-34 [sic] at Yorktown, Virginia in 1863." Two days later, the "second nine" whipped the Ninth Regiment 58-19. [23]

Robertson's *Soldiers Blue and Gray* also mentions a game in which the base runner had to be hit with the ball. "In one game between teams from the 13th Massachusetts and 104th New York, the Bay Staters won by a 66-20 score." [24]

On one occasion, a Union ball game encountered more action than they desired. Some Texas rebels opened fire on the Yankee outfielders. [25]

Immediately following the Civil War, the interest in baseball was obscured by the continual strife between the Radical Republicans in Congress and President Andrew Johnson. This acrimony dominated the newspapers. However, during the summer in 1866, a ray of hope appeared which would be a foretaste of good things to come.

Hudson, Ohio was an early hotbed of Base Ball, thanks in large measure to the "lads" at Western Reserve College. In June 1866, the Reserve Club challenged the Forest City Club of Cleveland, perhaps the premier team in northeast Ohio. The report of the game in the *Summit Beacon* presented a fine account of the action and the customary post-game camaraderie. However, it was more than a sports report by "OCULUS," the writer; it was a promotional piece for the College. The new physical education facility and the benefits of playing Base Ball were touted. Although some campus problems were frankly discussed, OCULUS would have been appalled if he had possessed the abilities of a Nostradamus and seen the campus problems of the future. Of particular pride to Western Reserve College was an alumnus and the new mathematics professor, Allen C. Barrows.

A. C. Barrows possessed marvelous athletic prowess, and he was the standout catcher for the Reserve nine. Even more impressive, but not noted in the newspaper article, was the fact that Barrows served as a 1st Sergeant in the 18th Regiment United States Infantry during the Civil War. The 18th U. S. was known for its tunneling and engineering skills. The regiment had marched with Gen. Don Carlos Buell to Shiloh and participated in the siege of Corinth. Among their many engagements were the major battles of Perryville, Stone River, Chickamauga, Mission Ridge at Chattanooga, Resaca, Dallas, Kenesaw Mountain, Atlanta, Franklin, and Nashville.[26] After the War of the Rebellion, A. C. Barrows was frequently requested to be a Base Ball umpire, which was certainly a wise decision. Not only was it ungentlemanly to argue with the umpire, but only a genuine cad would criticize such a gifted athlete and Civil War veteran.

What follows is an excellent sample of 1866 Americana.

Western Reserve College – Base Ball Match

The match game between the Forest City Club, of Cleveland, and the Reserve Club of Western Reserve College came off at Hudson on Saturday the 16th inst. [June] The weather was fine and cool, and the crowd assembled to see the playing was large.

The time set was 1-30 P.M. and play was called promptly at the hour, the Cleveland boys taking the bat.

In the first innings the splendid pitching of Mr. Ketchum and the powerful batting of the Clevelanders gave the latter 17 tallies. On the other hand when the Hudsonians took the bat, they found the Cleveland pitcher did not believe in giving much good balls, and as a result they made only three tallies. The decided superiority of the Forest City Club on the first innings was doubtless owing, in part, also to the fact that this was the first match game for the reserve Club and their excitement injured their playing. This gave the Clevelanders an advantage hard to be taken from them. The second innings the Hudson pitcher copied the Cleveland balls, and thenceforth the gain for Hudson was rapid until the 6th innings, when an unfortunate change of pitchers on the part of the Reserve Club, gave the others another start, and the final tally stood: Forest City 40; Reserve 26, - leaving the former just the advantage gained by the first innings.

The victory of the Clevelanders was decided but well earned, and had it not been for the fact that Harvey, one of the best men of the Reserve Club, was kept from playing by a sprained ankle and his place filled by a man from the "second nine" of Hudson, and for the facts above stated in regard to the pitching, the result would, to say the least, have been doubtful.

By an examination of the tables below, the comparative playing of the two clubs, and of the different numbers of each, can be seen. The following is the SCORE [sic]

[Reserve Club] Players	outs	runs	[Forest City Club] Players	outs	runs
Handford, 1b	4	3	Smith, c	1	6
Barrows, c	2	4	Hurlburt, ss	3	4
Bolton, lf	3	3	Clark, 1b	1	5
Curtiss, cf	3	3	McEwen, 2b	3	4
Hunker, ss	4	2	Eddy, lf	4	4
Ketchum, p	0	4	Vilas, 3b	4	5
Wilson, rf	3	2	Gorham, rf	3	4
Fitch, 3b	3	1	Stackley, p	2	4
Kennan, 2b	2	4	Miles, cf	3	4
Total	24	26		24	40

INNINGS

	1	2	3	4	5	6	7	8	Total
Reserve	3	4	7	1	3	1	0	7	26
Forest City	17	3	0	1	3	9	0	7	40

Umpire – J.M. Fisher, Penfield Club, Oberlin.

Scores – Tallman for the Reserve Club; Leffingwell for the Forest City Club.

The excitement of the crowd was lively, and vented itself by enthusiastic cheers whenever movement was particularly well executed. The applause seemed more enthusiastic towards the Reserve Club, though the fine play of the Forest City Club drew forth a good share of it.

After the game was over, the contesting clubs repaired to the College Library rooms, and did justice to a fine supper prepared and presided over by some of the young ladies of Hudson. – Then, after songs and speeches, the Clevelanders were accompanied to the station by the Reserve Club, and left for home amid the hearty cheers of the latter.

Before closing this notice, we beg leave, Mr. Editor, to say a few words in regard to the College. And first, we congratulate it on the erection of a Gymnasium, (limited, it is true) and on the introduction of Base Ball and other athletic games. In our College days, "Hole Marble" [27] was the rage, and the broad walk in front of the buildings was covered with excited players. Now it may be a fine thing to be able to "run the holes" or "kill" your antagonist at six feet distance, but we submit it, that "squatting" on a dirty walk and "knuckling down" are neither especially manly nor well calculated to develop muscles and impart physical vigor. Base Ball, however, gives vigorous exercise to all the principle muscles of the body and imparts vigor to the whole system. We hope the game will be kept up till the physical inferiority of Collegians ceases to be proverbial.

Second, we congratulate the College on the appointment of a *muscular* Professor, and on the fact that he is a graduate of the College. Prof. Barrows, who now fills the chair of Mathematics, loses nothing in the class room from the fact that he is the best player at the base, or that he can kick a foot-ball [sic] over the Chapel steeple some 90 feet in a vertical line. We should have alluded before to the splendid playing of the Professor, which drew such frequent applause at the match game. He acted as catcher and captain for the Reserve Club, and during the first two innings, we believe, caught all the men on "foul balls." His "fly catches" of foul balls were fine performances, and when he went around the scorers' tent and over two or three bystanders, and caught the ball before it struck the ground, the cheering was the loudest. [Since there were no mitts to catch the hard sphere, "fly catches" were duly appreciated by all.] Now the fact that the College has such a Professor encourages athletic sports, and this we think is a great advantage to the College.

Again, we rejoice that Mr. Barrows is an alumnus of the College, because it shows that the College *has confidence in itself.* So long as the Professorships were all filled from Yale or Dartmouth or Williams, people said, "If your own students are not good enough for Professors, your College is not good enough for us." Mr. Barrows is the first Professor appointed from the Alumni, for although Professor Gregory, the able and popular Principal of the Grammar School, went through most of his course at Hudson, he graduated at Harvard.

Third, one thing we are sorry to notice, the increased tendency to expensive habits among students. When young men or their parents have abundant means, and pay the regular College tuition (as *very* few do at Hudson) no one can question their right to dress expensively, hold fancy canes in their kidgloved hands, and give class and society suppers, if they keep College rules. And yet there is one objection. If they dress thus, and spend money thus, they (if in sufficient numbers) establish a certain style in college, which those who are not really able, feel that they must maintain. Again, the College is essentially a charitable institution, the small sum of $80

tuition per year would hardly half meet the current expenses of the institution, to say nothing of the cost of the grounds, buildings, and apparatus. All these were paid for by men who gave their money to found an institution to qualify men for the Christian Ministry. Many of these men were comparatively poor and gave their $500, more or less, when wheat was 50 cents per bushel, and butter 6 cents per pound. Now it is natural that these men should ask, "Did we deny ourselves and give our money to give tuition to young men that they may have the more money left for kid gloves, night suppers, and cigars?" We feel that this is an important matter. The college needs the sympathy and cordial support of its founders and early supporters. And the students should, we think, remember that its reputation depends in no small degree upon them. Especially do we think young men preparing for the ministry should look at this matter conscientiously. But a word to the wise is sufficient. In closing we must congratulate the college on its increased financial prosperity, on the ability of its Faculty, and on the increase in its number of student[s].
OCULUS [28]

As the pleasant summer days provided more Base Ball action, fan interest began to escalate, even though the game's procedures may have caused confusion as to what transpired. An example is the following letter to the *Western Reserve Chronicle* in Warren, Ohio in September of 1866. It may have been a tongue-in-cheek affair, or it was a truly confused account of a local game in Bristol of Trumbull County.

Sept. 10, 1866.
Mr. Editor : - As Base Ball Clubs are all the go, our young men determined not to be out done by their neighbors, have organized three clubs, one at the North Corners and two at the center. The club at the corners has been in *running* order for several weeks. – The clubs at the center have recently opened up; one is composed of young men, the other of "caques." Last Saturday the young men's club at the center, were called "from refreshments to labor" at one o'clock, P.M. -- We were honored with an invitation to the field and take a seat, and become a looker on, that is, witness the play. We did so, and I will give you what I learned on the occasion. The game being entirely new to most all present, the book on tactics had to be consulted first to find out how to lay off a field. This was done by

fixing four bases, ninety feet apart, in the form of a square. This done, tactics was again consulted to find out what was an innings and what was an outings. This important fact being established, the game commenced in earnest, which consisted principally in the players running with their greatest speed 360 feet, stopping three times to change their base. After waiting three hours to see where the *play* come in, I concluded the whole game required too much labor for me, inasmuch as I naturally incline to the lazy club of our neighboring town.

The score was now footed up, and I learned that one side had 64 innings, and the other side had 67 outings, and the Umpire decided that the outings had won the game by three majority.

GUEST. [29]

From August through September, the *Chronicle* gave thorough coverage to five games. Even "**Guest**" would have appreciated the account of the August 22 "Base Ball Match" between the Mahoning Base Ball Club of Warren and the Peerless Club of Sharon, Pennsylvania. [30]

Base Ball Match

Last Spring a base ball club was organized in Warren, consisting of some twenty odd members, who have met for a practice a number of afternoons of each week on the common south of the Canal. A few weeks age the first nine was selected, and was composed of the best players in the club. Lately their practice games have shown very good playing, the members each and all striving to do their best. When first organized, they gave themselves the name of "Mahoning Base Ball Club." Thinking they had attained sufficient proficiency in the game to do a little outside playing, they challenged the Peerless Club of Sharon, Pa., and a match was at once made. It came off in Warren last Saturday, P.M., on the grounds of Mrs. Gilbert, east of Red Run. At the time appointed both clubs appeared upon the ground, and tossed for choice, which was won by the Peerless, who sent the Mahoning to the bat. The game lasted about three hours, and was witnessed by a large number of persons from town, a goodly portion of whom were our fairest ladies, and resulted in the defeat of the Sharon boys by only one tally. Below we append a list of the score. A great deal of interest was manifested throughout the game by all the parties. The arrangements were admirable, and everything connected with the game was fairly conducted and gave satisfaction to all concerned. The Umpire, Mr. S. C. Iddings, of Warren, discharged his duties promptly and impartially, and won praises from both clubs. The pitching and catching of Hatfield and Harrington, of the Mahoning, and of Riddle and Hardy, of the Peerless, deserve special mention. — Vautrot of the Mahoning, as first base, was excellent. The finest playing by either club was done by Sherman – short stop – of the Mahoning. This young man has a lively way by getting over the ground, and freezing to the ball. Mahannah of the Peerless, as first base, was superior. The fielding of the Peerless boys was excellent, and they passed the ball to one another much more rapidly than the Mahoning boys. The Mahoning boys excelled in batting. The different Nines were well managed by their Captains, Hatfield of the Mahoning, and Hardy of the Peerless. The Peerless boys accepted their defeat gracefully, and anxiously wait for an opportunity to redeem themselves, which we understand they will soon have. In the evening, the Mahoning gave a supper to the Peerless club, at the "National." The Warren Silver Band was present, and discoursed excellent music. At nine o'clock the party sat down to the eatables, and every one present did ample justice to the good things before him. Quite a number of invited guests were present. After the supper had been disposed of, the company listened to appropriate remarks from C.G. Burton, E.P. Hatfield [both were Mahoning players] and others. The Sharon boys left for home shortly after ten o'clock, declaring themselves well satisfied with the treatment they had received in Warren.

MAHONING			PEERLESS		
Players	O.	R.	Players	O.	R.
Hatfield, p	5	0	Hardy, c	2	3
Harrington, c	5	1	Riddle, p	2	4
Sherman, ss	3	2	Wm. Ashton, ss	3	2
Vantrot, 1st b	2	3	Mahannah, 1st b	5	1
Smith, 2nd b	1	4	Mounts, 2nd b	4	2
Birchard, 3rd b	3	3	John Ashton, 3d b	2	3
Lanterman, l f	2	3	Haun, l f	5	1
Burton, c f	3	2	Gay, c f	0	1
Taylor, r f	3	2	Hughes, r f	4	2
Total	27	20	Total	27	19

[Completing the report were the box score and the following statistics: Fly Catches Made, Home Runs, Left On Base, Missed

Catches, and Passed Balls.]

The following week, "An interesting match was played between the Kinsman and Gustavus Clubs [both of Trumbull County]. ... Both were young Clubs, being organized the present summer, and this being the first match played by either Club." Kinsman prevailed 35-28 in a three-hour contest.

> The Umpire, Mr. Hawkins, showed himself thoroughly conversant with the game, and discharged his duties in a manner highly satisfactory to both Clubs. After the game was finished, a supper was served by Mr. Linsey, of the Kinsman Hotel, at the expense of the Gustavus Club, this being one of the stakes played for. The supper was got up in excellent style, and every one present did ample justice to the good things set before him.
> After the presentation of the ball by Capt. Bishop of the Gustavus Club [see Beadle's, Section One], the party broke up with the best of feelings.[31]

In late August, the Mahoning Club traveled to Bloomfield where the Warren boys were narrowly defeated by the home team, 21-20. Unbridled good sportsmanship reigned after the game ended.

> At the close of the game, the Bloomfield Club gave three cheers for the Mahoning Club, the Mahoning Club returning the compliment, three cheers were then given for the Umpire and three for the Scorers. The Bloomfield Club then gave the Mahoning Club and other guests a supper at Stevenson's Hotel which was no exception to his general rule of good meals for his customers.[32]

The team from Warren then had a rematch with the Peerless at Sharon, Pa.. The Peerless lived up to their name with a 55-35 victory. The teams combined for a total of 20 runs in the fifth inning. For the somewhat lopsided score, the *Chronicle* offered the following defense: "It is but due to the Mahonings to say that there were but five of its First Nine present, while the Peerless was out in full force." Still, the post-game ceremony was another pleasing affair. "In the evening the Warren boys were highly entertained, and after a well appreciated supper, at which appropriate remarks were made by Ash-

In the glow of the evening sunshine, the Akron Black Sox heartily give the three by three for their honorable opponents and the respected umpire, just as the Bloomfield Club and thousands of others cheered in days of yore: "Hip, hip, HUZZAH! Hip, Hip, HUZZAH! Hip, hip, HUZZAH!"

ton (P), Hatfield (M), and Burton (M), departed for home, well pleased with every thing and everybody."[33]

On September 8th, Kinsman and Gustavus had a rematch. Both teams juggled their lineups and added a new player or two. The correspondent to the *Chronicle*, who signed his name, "W," noted that "Mr. Woodworth, who is one of the best players in the Kinsman Club, was not present at the game, which showed itself plainly in the score." W's report shows the growing craze for baseball, the sportsmanship and camaraderie that was customary in this season, and W's sense of humor.

Base Ball in Gustavus

Gustavus, Sept. 8, '66

Editor Chronicle :

As the great national game of Base Ball is creating such an interest all over the country, the younger citizens of Gustavus, not to be behind the rest of the world, organized a Club about two weeks ago.

Having received a challenge from the Kinsman Club to play them a friendly game for the supper, we of course accepted it. – After a warmly contested game they beat us seven runs, and the natural result was, we had to draw our "weazel skins." Not being altogether satisfied with the result of the game, we challenged them to meet us on our own grounds and play for the same stakes....The game came off today in the presence of a large number of spectators ; no small few of which were ladies from this and the adjoining towns....

After an exciting game of about two hours and a half, the Gustavus Club was declared the victor by sixteen runs [43-27]. At the announcement of the result, the Gustavus boys gave three hearty cheers for the Kinsman Club which compliment was just as heartily returned; when both clubs united in complimenting the Scorers and Umpires.

At the conclusion of the game, the Captains of the respective clubs formed their men in line and marched over to Mr. L. Pelton's where a sumptuous repast awaited them. [Author's note: A precursor to the modern day trip to Dairy Queen?] After each one of the party had made several "fowl" catches of chicken pie and other good things, the score was read, and the ball presented by Captain Birrell of the Kinsman Club to Captain Roberts of the Gustavus Club.

A vote of thanks was unanimously tendered Mr. and Mrs.

Pelton for the excellent supper they had provided for us. After which the party broke up with many expressions of good will.

The Gustavus Cornet Silver Band was present and added much to the pleasure of the afternoon.... [34]

Back in Summit County and that hotbed of Base Ball in Hudson, the first "Mr. Octobers" were wrapping up the 1866 season.

PRIZE BASE BALL PLAYING.

Hudson, O. Oct. 7, '66

Eds. Beacon: – Will you please insert the following report of the Base Ball games in your columns, between the "Enterprise" and "Olympic" Base Ball Clubs of Hudson, for the $20 prize at Akron, Oct. 3, 1866, (played on the fair grounds.) The following clubs entered for the prize: "Freshman" class club of W. Reserve College, "Olympic" and "Enterprise" of Hudson, and "Summit" of Cuyahoga Falls. The "Summit" withdrew, after carefully measuring the ground. The "Freshmen" and the "Olympic" were first to go to bat. After a well played game the "Olympic" won the game by five tallies. In accordance with agreement the "Enterprise" took the bat against the "Olympic" and won the prize by four tallies [32-28]. [Single elimination tournaments were shunned, probably due to the time factor.]...

BALL PLAYER[35]

"Ball Player" included the lineups and scoring in his report. He briefly mentioned a game played on October 5th in Hudson between the "Excelsiors" of Cleveland and the "Enterprise." The Hudson boys romped to a 61-13 victory. Of particular note, J. Seymour, the Enterprise pitcher, scored ten times and made no outs. [36]

Baseball in northeast Ohio was on its merry way. Around the potbellied stoves of the general stores and other meeting places that winter, schemes and dreams were undoubtedly being discussed for the season of '67.

28

All eyes are on the flight of the ball; however, someone has eyes for the "Tally Lady" (Cathy Herald), who is waiting to tally the "aces" (runs).

CHAPTER THREE

THE SPIRIT OF THE GAME

In the springtime of 1867, the popularity of Base Ball began to spread like wildfire across the land. It would prove to be more than a game of physical prowess and enthusiastic play. A Base Ball match would be a social event, a source of community pride, and a love affair. It would be a magical season for Base Ball.

In the early spring the players and spectators had to familiarize themselves with some tinkering that was done to the rules. The *Summit Beacon* of Akron, Ohio printed the revisions, some of which seemed like mere reminders.

Base Ball

The following amendments to Base Ball rules published by the association will be read with interest by players.

1st. The pitcher's line is reduced from twelve to six feet.

2d. Balls bounding to the bat, going over the batman's head, or the side he does not strike from, are "unfair" balls, and must be called after warning.

3d. A jerked ball is one delivered by touching the side of the body arm. A thrown ball is one sent in with the body is bent. [sic] A pitched ball only can be sent in with a straight arm, swinging perpendicular.

4th. The striker is such only until he has hit a fair ball, then he becomes "a player running the bases."

5th. A balked or called ball is dead, and no player can be put out on it. Neither can the striker make a base on a balked ball, unless in case it be the third ball called.

6th. No batsman can be put out on three strikes if the third ball he strikes at be a balked or called ball: And no strike at such a ball is to be counted; and likewise no strike made purposely to strike out.

7th. The striker must have one foot on the line of his position when he hits the ball, and cannot take a step either backward or forward when striking at the ball.

8th. When the ball is stopped by the crowd, or spectators in any way, it becomes dead, and is not in play until the pitcher has held it while standing within the lines of his position.

9th. No player running home when two hands are out, can score his run if the batter be put out before making the first base.

10th. The Umpire must not only call all foul balls, but must call out how and by whom a player is put out. Thus if the striker be put out at first base, he must call out, " Striker out at first base."

14th. All persons who play for money are called "professional players," and as such cannot play in any match played by any association club; and any Umpire learning that such a player is in a nine in a match in which he is acting, must at once call "time," insist on the professional being removed from the nine, or resign his position as Umpire, thereby making the game "null and void." [37]

Baseball has always had a sense of humor, and those who played and watched the game of 1867 could good-naturedly poke fun at themselves as this article from the *Harrisburgh Patriot* exhibits. [38]

New Rules for Base Ball
From the Harrisburgh Patriot.

The Tyrolean Base Ball Club of this city, having become demoralized by the recent contest, has adopted the following rules, which they recommend to the fraternity everywhere.

1. No one weighing over 300 pounds will be allowed to play.

2. Express wagons will be on hand to carry the players from base to base.

3. No player will be allowed more than three men to help him to his home base.

4. Any player occupying more than fifteen minutes in going from one base to another will be counted out.

5. Persons residing within half a mile of the grounds are requested to close their shutters to prevent accidents.

6. Spectators are not allowed within twenty feet of the bat.

7. Owners of horses hitched within half a mile of the grounds must be responsible for all accidents that may occur to their "animules."

8. Men without arms or legs can not become members.

9. Players can stop for refreshments at each base, where a

small bottle will be found. This bottle is sometimes called a *base vial*.

    10. Hogs and cattle will not be allowed to pasture on the playing ground during the game.

    11. Fielders will carry their *vials* with them, in order to avoid the necessity of coming in for drinks.

    12. Scorers will not be allowed extra drinks on that score.

    In spite of its sense of humor and its attempt to be a gentleman's game, Base Ball was an energetic game which had its risks. Perhaps this element of danger attracted these Americans also.

    In a match between Kinsman and Gustavus in the previous year, " At the close of the third Innings, Hatch of the Gustavus Club being disabled, was compelled to leave the field, and as no substitute could be found the game was finished with eight players." [39]

    In 1867, the injury bug was still biting the Gustavus team. It happened in an early June game between the Independent Club of Gustavus and the Farmers Club of Bristol. "But a few bats were made before M. D. Powell, occupying left field, in attempting to take a fly ball, received a complicated dislocation of a finger, which disabled him for further play. Mr. Hathaway, a younger member, was sent to the position." [40]

    Handling that leather-covered, India rubber ball must have played havoc with the hands and fingers, but only a sissy would think of wearing a glove for protection. The first recorded use of a glove was in 1875 when a Boston first baseman, Charles C. Waite, made himself a glove because his hands were banged up. He was ashamed to wear the glove, however, and he made it a flesh color hoping that it would go unnoticed. Poor Charles was ridiculed for being a member of the "kid glove aristocracy." [41]

    Eight years before Waite's pinkish glove, the boys on Akron's team certainly were not of the kid glove aristocracy.

    At the drill of the Akron Base Ball Club on Tuesday, John Buchtel butted heads with another player, on a "catch," with such force as to seriously injure one of his eyes, and render it necessary for his companions to assist him in getting home. Several other similar accidents have happened of late. Wins. [sic] Babcock having the skin and ligaments between the thumb and index finger badly lacerated a few days since, by a flying ball that he was endeavoring to catch. [42]

The *Portage County Democrat* reported other dangers to the boys of '67. [43]

Base Ball in a New Aspect.

The treasurer of a Wisconsin base ball club made a quarterly report which is a model for minute accuracy. Some of the items give a few of the unpleasant features of the noble pastime, in whose pursuit there are involved more or less dangers to clothes and limbs. We give these items as they are printed in a Wisconsin exchange:

H.S. Claur, for repairing rent in breeches of member of first nine, caused by squatting to catch fly-ball..........................$1.00.

Dr. Dalton, for setting thumb of member of first nine........60.

Dr. Dalton, for extracting splinter of bat from shin of member of second nine..1.00.

Dr. Dalton, for one quart of solution eye-wash.............3.00.

R.D. Pulford, druggest, one ounce chloroform for use of member of second nine, to have his knee-pan taken off to have contusion scraped off...1.00.

T.W. Murphy, harness-maker, for sewing up slit in ear of member of first nine..50.

Dr. Moffat, druggest, three yards coarse [gauze?]...........40.

Then there was a game in Akron where "Kline applied for an ambulance to reach home; - having his full of 'ye noble game.' Smith made a 'home run' before the game was closed – had enough." [44]

Regardless of the risks involved, many people from different walks of life and of a wide range of ages were ready for the fray. It was to be a season with a variety of games.

On the political scene, you know that something is good when the politicians try getting their hands into the action. The *Porage County Democrat*, actually a Republican oriented newspaper, reported the following action at Kent, Ohio.

Base Ball – Political Game—Republicans Win. –

A friendly game of Base Ball was played on Saturday upon the grounds of the Island Club, of Kent, between the Republican nines, under W. W. Patton, Captain, and Democratic nines, under C. P. Kelso, Captain. None of the players had ever played a game before, which was a large element in the fun of the occasion. At the end of seven even innings, the Republican nine were declared the victors by thirteen tallies. A fine supper was served the players at the Franklin House at the expense of the defeated players. [45]

The play of the politicians might have been inept, but that of some youth teams evoked expressions of admiration. A gentleman using the name of "Obediah" reported the following to the *Western Reserve Chronicle*:

> A match game was played at Bristol, by two Junior clubs, boys from about 12 to 14 and 15 years old. One of the clubs of Bristol, the other of Bloomfield, the sharpest game I have ever heard of. Score – Bloomfield 14 – Bristol 10. Five whitewashes on one side and two or three on the other. Who can beat this? [46]

Another youth game was reported under the heading, "Juvenile Base Ball."

> There are in Kent and Ravenna, Juvenile Base Ball Clubs, composed of lads of thirteen to sixteen years of age. Imitating the example of their "big brothers" the two clubs played a match game at Kent on Saturday [Oct. 26]. The Kent club chose for its name "Active," the Ravenna juveniles sporting the title "Star Club Junior." The match game was a very pleasant one, and was played with all due regard to the rules and regulations, in such cases, made and provided. The "Stars Junior" were the victors of the field by a score 118 to 19 and came home with all the pride of victors and were received with shouts and cheers by their young associates. [47]

On the collegiate scene, the players at Hiram vied for the title of "Boys of October." It was the same glorious Saturday on which the "Stars Junior" were the victors over the Kent "Active."

> On Saturday the 26th inst., two friendly match games were played between the Delphic and Hesperian Societies of this place. Everything passed off lively and pleasantly with of course the usual amount of good and bad playing on both

sides. The score stood in the first game, Hesperian 24, Delphic 19. In the second, Hesperian 27, Delphic 11. [48] [Judging from the length of time to play a game in this age, the college boys may have played for seven hours on this late autumn Saturday.]

Manufacturing concerns also fielded teams in 1867. It appeared to be a win-win situation for the factory owners. Their employees gained the benefits of Base Ball playing and perhaps pride in their establishment. The companies also garnered free advertising when their game results were printed in the newspapers. An example is the following game that was played in early September.

Base Ball. – The propriators and employees of the "Unions," (Johnson and Baldwin,) and the "Museum," (Viall & Ruckels's) Stoneware Manufacturies, played a "muffin" game of base ball on the grounds of the Mechanics' Club in Middlebury [now part of east Akron] on Saturday, September 7th, resulting in victory for the latter by a score of 111 to 47. [This is the game after which Smith (r.f.) and Kline (2nd baseman) were the worse for wear. The two men gave it their all even though their team was whomped. Smith scored 8 times and Kline crossed the plate for 5 runs.] [49]

As for the playing atmosphere of the game in 1867, there are many newspaper accounts. Herein are five of the best reports that this author found which illustrate the camaraderie and sportsmanship that existed between the players and their communities as well as the general aura of the occasion.

The first article concerns an unusual game between the employees of the insane asylum and a nearby team. The atmosphere and conduct of the game appeared to be of greater interest to the reporter than the outcome of the game itself. The fact that the Asylum Club defeated the Iron Club by a score of 49-29 seemed to be an afterthought.

Base Ball at Newburgh

Newburgh, July 7th, 1867.

It is a fact worthy of comment and pleasant to note, that Newburgh is alive and stirring this hot, sultry weather, as was amply illustrated last Saturday afternoon, by a well-contested game of Base Ball for the Prize Bat, between the "Iron Club," composed of athletic young men selected from the promising of our flourishing village, and the "Asylum Club," composed of the employees of one of the noblest institutions that ever blessed the country. The game was played upon the grounds of the "Asylum Club," back of the Institution, and resulted in a complete victory in their favor, as will be seen consulting the subjoined report. The grounds were thronged by a large concourse of the good citizens of Newburgh, of both sexes, and all ages, for whose accommodation and ease comfortable seats were placed in the cool, shady places, wherever the weary frame might rest, while the ever-watchful, active mind was enjoying the excitement of the deeply interesting game. Among the spectators the *patients* were not the least interested. Many of the female patients were present, with their attendants, and as the game was in full view of the male wards, all the windows were filled with eager watchers. Whenever anyone was unusually successful it was highly appreciated by them, as was manifested by the cheerful laugh and sharp witticism perpetrated at the expense of the more unfortunate party. We understand that daily games of this healthful and athletic exercise are indulged, and taken part in, by the patients, for their especial benefit and amusement.

Each member of both Clubs proved himself an honor to his respective Club. Much praise is due the Umpire, Mr. Griffith of the "Star Club" for the faithful, efficient and impartial manner in which he discharged the unpleasant duties of his honorable position. The Captains displayed exquisite generalship in bringing their men to the "home base."

The success of each player is truthfully represented in the following synopsis or report of the game.

The three cheers so heartily given in honor of the Scorers, were richly merited.

The best of feeling prevailed among all parties during the entire game.

The "Iron Club" challenged the "Iron Club" to another contest on the afternoon of July 12th, which was promptly accepted by the latter...[50]

In a second example where the aura of the game overshadowed the results, the writer, who was a member of the Akron team, not only eliminated the rosters and the statistics, but also the score of the game.

B. B. – Akron vs. Canton.

Editor Beacon: On Thursday, the 25th of July, last, the "Akrons," as per arrangement, played a friendly game of Base Ball with the "Starks," of Canton. The game commenced at half past two o'clock in the afternoon, and was obliged to be called at the end of fifth innings, on account of the rain – the "Akrons" coming out victorious. The "Starks" labored under the disadvantage of having two or three of their first nine away, and in consequence did not play their usual game. A pleasanter game than the one played at Canton with the "Starks" the "Akrons" never played. Their treatment, at the hands of the "Starks" not only, but by the citizens generally, was most courteous and generous, and the "Akrons" felt that they were among friends and gentlemen, who although they were their antagonists on the ball grounds, understood and practiced the laws of hospitality in their fullest sense. In the evening the "Akrons" were invited to the house of Col. Schneider, Representative for Stark County, where they met a few of the Canton "belles," and passed the time most delightfully until 11 o'clock. One of the "Akrons," who is verging on "old bachelorhood," remarked that any young man who could live in Canton and be content to live an old bachelor, must be *non compos mentis*. We think so, too.

It is not definitely settled when the "Starks" will come to Akron to play the return game.

"FIRST NINER." [51]

The reporter took a different approach for the game between the Mahoning Club of Warren and the Independent Club of Gustavus. The initial stress was on the complete rosters and statistics in the game that was won by Gustavus, 32-25. Stating that "We have not space to give the full details," the editor reconsidered and added the game analysis after the statistical report.

> ... The first two or three innings of the game were about as sharply played as any we ever saw, but after that the game was not carried on with the spirit of the outset. The batting on

either side was not as heavy as that generally done in that part of the country, but was well up to that of most match games. Barnes, of the Independent, made the only home run, and that was on bad throwing.

After the game was over, both sides, preceded by the band, adjourned to an adjacent grove, where a splendid pic nic [sic] supper had been prepared by the ladies of Gustavus, who appeared to take as much interest in base ball as the men did, and as heartily eschew the intensely invigorating (?) game of croquet as they would that of playing billiards. The players did ample justice to the supper, and after the presentation of the ball by the umpire, to Capt. Barnes, of the Independent, the presentation of boquets [sic], speeches, &c., the crowd adjourned, all feeling as well as could be expected under the circumstances.... [52]

The fourth example of the game's aura in 1867 clearly illustrates the close proximity of the spectators to the playing action. The situation must have been comical at times and quite frustrating at other moments, as the Farmers Club of Bristol dueled the Independent Club of Gustavus. [53]

... The playing was generally good, and many times close and interesting. The batting on both sides was excellent, very balls striking inside the field. Everything passed off smoothly, and the best feeling was maintained between the contesting parties. The good feeling existing between Capt's House, of the Farmers, and Barnes, of the Independent, their management of the players, and their excellent playing, are worthy of special remark.

There was one feature, however, which detracted from the harmony of the occasion, and that was the carelessness or imprudence of many of the spectators in crowding upon the Scorers, conversing with the Umpire, as well as obstructing the movements of the fielders.

At the close of the game, cheers were given for each Club, the Umpire and Scorers, and for Capt. Barnes. We then partook of a refreshing supper given by the Independent. The ball furnished by the Farmers was then given up to the winning club.... [Incidentally, the Independent Club defeated the

Farmers Club in a thriller, 52-50, which lasted three and half hours. The duration of the game might have been reduced with better crowd control, but what would have been the fun in that? An interesting note is that the lineups were matched by fielding positions.]

Farmers Club			Independent Club		
Players	O	R	Players	O	R
Fenton, c	2	7	Barnes, c	3	7
House, p	2	8	Morey, p	0	7
Loomis, s s	2	8	Cowden, s s	2	6
Fenton, 1 b	5	4	Brainard, 1 b	3	6
Sager, 2 b	1	7	Hart, 2 b	2	7
Parker, 3 b	2	5	Case, 3 b	4	5
Mayhew, l f	4	4	Hathaway, l f	3	5
Barb, c f	6	2	Whiston, c f	5	3
White, r f	3	5	Baily, r f	4	4

The fifth example further illustrates the enthusiasm without the attitude. This was not a time of in-your-face confrontations, do-your-own-thing gyrations, finger-pointing, or crotch-grabbing players. This time the Farmers Club of Bristol were outscored by the Grand River Club of Austinburg, the latter scoring 26 runs in the last two innings to pull away to a 64-41 triumph. Nevertheless, the Farmers were excellent hosts.

After the game was duly decided, the Farmers invited the Grand River boys to the house of Jacob Sager, where was found a table plentifully decorated with everything that is pleasant to the taste, and to which all decided ample justice was done. Having duly refreshed themselves, all dispersed for the night. At 9 o'clock on the following morning the Grand River boys took their departure, feeling very favorably with Trumbull County, and especially of Bristol, and fully appreciating the many kindnesses received at their hands. [54]

There may have been a unique blend of sportsmanship and camaraderie in the baseball season of 1867; however, all was not peace and harmony. After all, Base Ball was a competitive endeavor; and within that endeavor there were people who loved to win – some more so than others. So if one were to suffer a slit ear, a damaged kneecap, torn clothing, and an aching and bruised body, then it would at least be more gratifying to walk or limp away with the joy of victory.

In addition to the love of winning, there was the quest to see who had the best team. (Since it has been intimated that gambling was a problem for Base Ball in the 1860's, gamblers certainly had an interest in knowing which was the best team.) Eventually, the powerhouse teams challenged each other, which was a process of determining who was the best. Toward the end of the season, tournaments were held wherein a team could see if it was the best nine and perhaps to gain regional recognition and local fame.

Since professionalism was abhorred, the individuals could only lay claim to the intangible aspects of victory in the tournaments. However, the **team** could earn prize money. Whether any of the prize money filtered down to the players, certainly no one was going to say.

Of several tournaments that fall, an unusual one was held at Twinsburg. The extra attractions gave it the essence of a school's field day.

> **Base Ball Tournament.** – A grand base ball tournament is announced to take place at the Twinsburg Fair Grounds on the 17th and 18th of October. A purse of $100 is offered for the best nine; $30 for the beaten clubs; $25 for those clubs that have been organized over five months. Prof. Barrows of Hudson College is to act as Umpire. Upon the first day a grand sack race will take place at 1 P.M. for a prize of $10. On the second day a purse of $15 for the three best lady equestrians, and also a purse of $15 for a foot race, best two in three once around the track. [55]

The quest to be the best was sooner or later destined to lead to some bad blood between the powerhouse teams.

(Top) Shane "Lefty" Gault checks the cowbell, the ringing of which will signal the scoring of an ace. (Bottom) Dave Eiermann of the Akron Black Sox lays out for a "daisy cutter," [a hot grounder]

CHAPTER FOUR

THE FEUD

In 1867, the horizons for the urban citizens were much broader, especially their Base Ball horizons. Thanks to their magic carpet made of steel, the towns and cities along the railroad were not limited to dusty crossroads competition. With the "Iron Horse' expanding the playing areas of Base Ball hotbeds like Akron, Hudson, and Cleveland, the quest to be the best was in earnest. Yet, in the early spring no one could foretell what a terrific Base Ball season was in store for the enthusiasts.

Some odd news came across the telegraph wires in the merry month of May. First, "Over a dozen bodies have been fished out of the river at Chicago within three weeks." Second, a Portland man committed suicide because "He had been married a short time previous and it wore upon his mind." Then there was the case of the female cook on a canal boat in the Erie basin. She "threw oil in the fire from a can. The flames set her clothing on fire. Her screams attracted a couple of men, who instantly pitched her into the canal." Needless to say, the cook was in poor condition. Of more importance, however, was the first high-powered Base Ball match of the 1867 season.[56]

The Hudson "Olympics" club was touted as the third best nine in Summit County, and they invited the Cleveland "Occidental" to town. There could be no fingernails left after this *five-hour* nail-biter. As will be seen, the playing field was adorned by one of those delightful idiosyncrasies of the day; and as usual, the Hudson correspondent threw in some non-Base Ball items.

Hudson ---Base Ball---Match Game.

Hudson, May 18th, 1867.

Mr. Editor: -- Our first base ball match of this season (if we except the one at the Seminary) was played on the grounds of the Reserve, between the Occidentals, of Cleveland, and the Olympics, of the Preparatory Department of W.R.C. At an early hour, a large number had assembled from the town and country, and we observed some from your town (beg your pardon, we mean your city) to witness the game. At a match game between these same clubs a year ago, the Occidentals had won by one tally, and a close contest was expected. At two o'clock the Olympics went to the bat, the Occidentals winning the choice and taking the field. The game lasted until 7 o'clock. The following is the score:

[With a 7-run ninth inning rally, the Olympics pulled out a 41-38 decision. The box score was a little different from previous ones. The usual columns for runs (R) and outs made (O) came first. Then there was a column for flies caught (F.C.) and missed flies (M.F.).]

The unenvied office of umpire was filled by W. Scales, of the Forest City Club. His decisions were prompt and satisfactory. The Occidentals took the lead and kept it until the last inning. They went to work with a will and seemed even too confident of success. – The company who came from Cleveland became exultant over their continued good fortune, and some found it necessary to climb a hay stack to find room to give vent to their unbounded joy. The whitewash cooled them down somewhat, but they were confident to the end. The Olympics were not so enthusiastic as their opponents, in the first part of the game. They were not far behind, however, and at the beginning of the last inning were within 3 of being even. The last inning was intensely exciting. Every movement was cheered by one side or the other; but fortune favored the Olympics, who won by 3 tallies. A challenge has been given for another game, but no arrangements have been made as yet.

The long contested tax for a new school has at last been carried, the sum being $5000. [This is not a typo.]

The fruit has not been injured by the frost, and there are indications of a large crop this season.

More anon, CITIZEN [57]

The intense competition between the Olympics and the Occidentals signaled a shift in values for the "big time" Base Ball clubs. Although still important, sportsmanship and the physical values of playing the game began to take a back seat to winning the "big game" and acquiring bragging rights. In the process, the seeds of a Base Ball feud were sowed on June 19th when two of the best teams in the area clashed in a "friendly game of Base Ball."

The "Akrons" traveled to Hudson to play the "Reserves." The game began at 2:40 that spring day. The "Reserves" jumped into an early lead and were in command after seven innings, 37-28. Then, the "Akrons" rallied for 18 runs in the 8th inning and 7 more in the 9th. After three hours and 20 minutes of intense competition, the "Akrons" pulled out a 53-41 victory. [58]

Nothing of import was mentioned in the *Summit Beacon*'s game report, just the bare facts and the statistics. However, as later events proved, some bad feelings remained when the game was over.

Although the Reserves had to feel disheartened about their collapse in the last two innings of the Akron game, the Hudson boys managed to regain their composure and to exert a terrific effort against the Cleveland powerhouse, the Forest City Club.

An unnamed Cleveland *Daily Leader* chronicler penned a literary masterpiece worthy of any baseball era. The writer imparted a history lesson on the Forest City Club's prize bat and ball, presented a philosophical outlook on life – at least Base Ball life – and a picturesque description of a day worth living and remembering. A tightly contested and skillfully played game certainly aided the Base Ball writer's spectacular journalistic endeavor. This classic game report is presented in its entirety.

BASE BALL
Match Game for the Prize Ball and Bat, between the Reserve Club of Hudson, and Forest City, of Cleveland – The Former Victorious by one Run.

We sit in sackcloth and ashes, lamenting for the glory that has departed from us! With a bolt of crape enshrouding our sanctum, we "wipe our weeping eyes" as we chronicle the fact that the Forest City base ball Club, which we thought invincible, and which for almost a year has held the prize ball and bat against all opposers, and maintained their reputation and the honor of our city on all occasions, has at last been fairly beaten. The Hudson boys have " bearded the lion in his den," and after a brilliant contest, come out conquerors, and borne away to their classic shades the coveted symbols of victory which have been the cynosure of the eyes of many an aspiring club. Our pencil is loth to record the result of the match yesterday, but we will endeavor to yield to the force of circumstances as gracefully as did the members of the Forest City Club at their defeat, and accord the meed of praise to the gentlemanly *athletes* of Western Reserve College.

The first match for the ball and bat was played on the 4th of July, 1866. The prize was offered by a number of gentlemen of this city for a match between the Forest City of Cleveland, and the Penfield of Oberlin, the winning club to hold the ball and bat for one year against all challenges from the Western Reserve [referring to the region of northeast Ohio], not being compelled, however, to play more than once in thirty days for the prize. The first match resulted in a victory for the Forest City by a score of 48-14, in eight innings. The second match was between the same clubs, and was played Saturday, August 25th [1866] resulting in a victory to the Forest City by a score of 86-18, in nine innings. The third was played October 12th [1866], between the champions and the Railway Union Club, and resulted in a victory to the champions by a score of 28-26, in seven innings. The fourth game was with the same club played May 30th [1867], in which the Forest City Club "held their position" by a score of 67-26. The fifth match was that of yesterday [June 28]. Had the Forest City held the prize seven days longer they would have been entitled to it, hereafter, in fee simple, but the fates – i.e. the Hudson boys – had decided otherwise, and the result is before us. A match game between these two clubs was played at Hudson, in May, 1866, which resulted in a victory for the Forest City by a score of 40-26. This fact, coupled with the brilliant prestige of subsequent conquests, no doubt led many to accept it as a foregone conclusion that the Reserves would return as empty handed as they came, and indeed, it is probable that the Forest City Club anticipated an easy victory, but the "best laid schemes o' base ball players , as well as other men, "gang oft agley."

The game yesterday was one of the most brilliant and closely contested ever played in this city, as will be evinced by the score. The weather was all that could have been desired. The heat of the sun was not intense and a gentle breeze tempered the atmosphere just to the right degree for comfort. The Forest City boys, with their usual courtesy and forethought, had put the ground in good condition and prepared ample accommodations for spectators. None would have thought, a few years ago, that our whole community could be so deeply interested in a subject which, at first thought, seems so trivial as base ball, gradually however, it has insinuated itself into the public mind until our "crack club" has become the pride of the city, and there is not one who does not feel a jealous pride in the record it has made. All have rejoiced at its success, and now that its banner trails, all will experience a feeling of regret.

The game was set at half-past three o'clock, but long before that hour the Kinsman street cars were crowded with passengers, and vehicles of all descriptions, including scores of gay Euclid avenue "turnouts" with dashing steeds and liveried jehus, the cushioned seats of which were pressed by the very *elite* of the city, thronged the streets leading to the grounds. It is well known that the ladies are passionate admirers of athletic displays, and it will not be wondered at that silk and dimity comprised a large proportion of the vast concourse assembled to witness the game. The crowd numbered fully three thousand, and from first to last the most intense enthusiasm and interest was manifested. Little girls in pinafores, and five-year-old urchins with the first pair of boots, shared in the general feeling. They seemed to fully comprehend the game and the situation, and their little hands clapped in glee and their bright eyes sparkled when a fine play was made. Of course the Forest City boys were the favorites with the spectators, although they were quite as ready to applaud the skill of the Reserves. The Railway Union boys and their friends were there in large numbers, and as they were in the same relation to the coveted prize that the fox was to the grapes in the Aesopian fable, they were in full sympathy with the Hudson boys, and freely indulged in the most extraordinary declarations regarding their intentions in the event of the defeat of the Forest City.

The game was called at 3:45, and the Forest City, winning the choice, took the field.

FIRST INNING

Barrows, of the Reserve, went to the bat and was immediately caught out on a "foul." Hunker followed, meeting a precisely similar fate. Kennan made a fine strike to center field, but was caught out on a "fly" by Clark, thus closing the first inning of the Reserves, with a most inauspicious "whitewash."

Capt. Smith, of the Forest City, made a splendid stroke, reaching the first base easily, and came home on the three balls following, without difficulty, scoring the first tally. Clark followed, and was caught out on three misses. McEwen and Hurlburt easily scored tallies. Scates struck a fine blow, but it was caught "on the wing" by Kennan and he retired in good order. Truesdale came in "O. K." but Stockley was caught out on a fly by Barrows, closing the inning. Score – Forest City, 4; Reserve, 0.

SECOND INNING

The result of the first was a trifle disheartening, but the Reserves solaced themselves with the time-honored maxim that "a game is never out till it is played out," and went confidently to the bat. Smith by a good stroke made the second base. While Harvey was batting, on account of bad pitching, the Reserve gained a base by three "balls." Haskell followed with a splendid stroke reaching second base, and bringing home Smith and Harvey. Brooks easily made first base, and second on a stroke of Harrington. The latter, however, couldn't get up speed enough to make the base, and was put out by Clark. Williams followed and another base was gained by bad pitching, Harrington coming home. Williams, Barrows and Hunkers each made a score, but the fates were less propitious to Kennan, and through the agility of Stockley was put out on first base. Harvey was caught out on a fly, sending the Reserves to the field, after a fine score of seven tallies.

Gorham, of the Forest City, took the bat, made first base, and easily came home on a passed ball. Brown and Smith made third and second bases, respectively, when Clark was again sent to the retired list by a well caught fly. McEwen made a splendid stroke, narrowly escaping the fate of Clark, but the fly was missed and he succeeded in making second base, bringing home Brown and Smith. Hulburt went out in a foul, caught by Harvey. McEwen and Truesdale made time, when Stockley was put out on first, giving the bat to the Reserves, after five tallies. Score: Forest City 9, Reserve 7.

THIRD INNINGS [sic]

Haskell went to the bat and "made his mark" but Brooks and Harrington were "unlucky," the former "going to grass" on first base and the latter on a foul. William's stroke brought in Haskell and himself to second base. Barrows made a splendid blow to right field, Clark "went for it" right gallantly, but made a "missed fly" and Williams came home. Barrows went out while struggling for second base on Hunker's stroke, closing the inning with two tallies.

Gorham of the Forest City went out in a foul, Brown followed with a tally; Smith and Clark made third and second, when McEwen went out on a fly caught by Smith. Hulburt brought in Smith and Clark, and Truesdale reciprocated by letting him in. Before he could "scrutch" his run, however, Scates was sent belowon a fly by Kennan closing the third innings with four tallies. Score: Forest City 13, Reserve 9.

FOURTH INNING

Hunker went to bat and easily made his point. Kennan went out on first base; Smith scored one, and Harvey was "laid out" by Clark on first. Haskell and Brooks easily scored, when Clark slaughtered Williams on the first base, closing the inning with four tallies, making the score even on odd innings.

Stockley made a powerful strike with evident good intentions, but Haskell made a fine fly catch and the batter went under the umbrella. Gorham, Brown and Smith easily tallied, when Clark made his third base on a splendid strike, but before he could get home, McEwen was caught out on a foul fly by Harvey, and Hulburt on a fly by Barrows, closing the fourth inning with three tallies. Score, Forest City 16, Reserve 13.

FIFTH INNING

This opened decidedly inauspiciously for the Reserves, Barrows going out at once on a foul and Hunker on a fly, beautifully caught by McEwen. Kennan was more fortunate, and after making his first base on his own, came home on Smith's stroke. Smith and Harvey succeeded in scoring, when Harrington was put out on the first base by the inevitable Clark, with Brooks and Haskell on bases. The Reserves made three tallies, evening the score – sixteen each – the Forest City having the advantage of the inning.

Truesdale of the Forest City went into the shade on a foul. Scates made his tally easily, and Stockley took the bat, but having been partially crippled in the early part of the game by a ball which struck his foot, McEwen in the capacity of "legs" for him. Stockley made a fine stroke, and Mac "lit out," making his run easy. Brown struck a good blow, but was caught on a splendid fly-catch by Kennan, closing the fourth [fifth] inning with two tallies. Score: Forest City 18, Reserve 16.

SIXTH INNING

Harvey, the catcher of the Reserves, had met with an accident, his hand having been injured by the ball, and Harrington took his place, Harvey taking the "short stop." Williams took the bat but went down on a foul; Barrows scored, when Hunker was knocked out of time by Clark on first ball.

Kennan marked one, evening the score for the third time, when Smith became another of Clark's victims at first base.

The Forest City took the bat, Smith scoring an easy tally. Clark made first base, when McEwen by a splendid stroke sent the ball spinning along the ground to left field with great velocity. Clark came easily home, followed closely by Mac, who reached the home amid a storm of applause from the spectators, having made the first home run of the game. Hurlburt imitating his example did likewise, owing, however, to the awkward fielding as well as his own agility. Truesdale and Scates made their tallies, when Gorham, Brown and Smith were put out in succession, closing the sixth innings with six runs. Score, Forest City 24, Reserve 18.

SEVENTH INNINGS [sic]

Harvey took the bat and made first base. Haskell followed with a splendid stroke, bringing Harvey home, and himself to second. Brooks did a like favor for Harvey, and Harrington for Brooks, making his own tally without difficulty. The fdates then frowned again upon the classic club, and Williams and Barrow went out, the former on first base, and the latter by a foul, nicely caught by Smith. Hunker and Kennan made their tallies by fleet running, but Smith was unlucky again, and went out on a foul, giving the bat to Forest City. They made six tallies, again placing the score even on odd inning – 24 each.

Clark went to the bat and made an easy score. McEwen was floored by a foul beautifully caught by Harrington. When Stockley took the bat Hurlburt was on third base, Truesdale on second and Scates on first. The two former came in on a passed ball, and Scates shortly after. Stockley made his third base and Gorham his second, when a fly from Brown was finely caught by Kennan, who by splendid double play immediately passed the ball to second base, laying out Gorham and closing the inning with five tallies. Score, Forest City 29, Reserve 24.

EIGHTH INNING

Harvey took the bat, but at once retired, McEwen making a fine fly catch. Haskell, who up to this time had the only clean score on either side, was unlucky in this inning and went out on a foul.

At this stage the prospects were most unfavorable for the Reserves, as they had two men out, and one inning to follow, while the Forest City had before them two full innings and were, besides, five tallies ahead. Yet the Reserves were undaunted, and Brooks went boldly to bat. He made a good stroke, and by fine running reached third base in two following balls. They narrowly escaped a second "whitewash," Harrington barely reaching first base. Brooks, Harrington, Williams, Barrows and Hunker all scored, when Kennan went down by an excellent fly-catch by Truesdale. For the fifth time the score was placed even on odd innings – 29 each.

Smith made an easy run for the Forest City, Brown and Clark made third and second bases when McEwen went out on a foul-fly, caught by Brooks, Brown went home and Clark to third on a passed ball. Hurlburt followed up a fine strike and very nearly made a home run, the ball crossing the home-base an instant before him. Truesdale went out on a foul fly caught by Harrington, and Scates on a fly well caught by Kennan, closing the innings with four tallies. Score: Forest City, 33; Reserve 29.

NINTH INNING

At this point the excitement of the crowd became most intense. Unless the Reserves made more on the average on former innings it seemed that nothing would save them from defeat. The friends of the Forest City were jubilant, while the Railway boys and the Hudsoners, in low, earnest tones invoked the angel who presides over the destinies of base-ball matches. It looked dark enough when Smith was shelved immediately by Clark on first base.

Harvey made his second base on a good stroke and by watching his opportunity reached home in safety. Haskell and Brooks made second and third bases, when both were brought in by a fine stroke from Harrington who made his second base. The bases were all occupied by Barrows, Harrington and Williams, when Hunker made a fine stroke which brought home the first two. Kennan next went out in a foul. Smith narrowly escaped being caught out on a fly by Hurlburt, but succeeded in reaching home. Harvey was put out on home base while striving gallantly to reach it, closing the books for the Reserves with eight tallies in the last inning, placing them 37 – 4 ahead of the Forest City.

The excitement of the eager throng was now wonderful. Every motion was most anxiously watched, and the result of each stroke evoked the wildest applause from either one side or the other.

To his teammates' chorus of "Leg it! Leg it! Leg it!" the Chagrin Falls "Forest Citys" runner breaks for second base. "One Bounce" Searl covers 1st base for the Black Sox.

The Forest City played with extreme caution, for it was very evident they had not a "sure thing" of it. They must score five to win, and every player nerved himself up to do the best in his power. The Reserves, also, seeing the prize so nearly their own, were no less earnest, and the inning was one of intense interest. Stockley made a score, when Gorham was caught out on a fly by Haskell. This caused loud applause, and we heard one enthusiastic youth from Hudson declare that if they could beat them he would gladly give every cent he had and sleep all night in the lock-up! Brown reached home in safety, but Clark was slaughtered on his own base, where he had "laid out" so many of the Reserves. Smith scored a tally making three, when McEwen, by an unlucky stroke, was caught on a fly by Barrows, closing the game, and giving the Reserves the victory by one tally. It is impossible to describe the scene that followed. The air was filled with caps, palm leafs and even glossy tiles, and shouts of triumph went up from the Reserves and their friends. The Railway boys rushed in, and embraced them affectionately, giving vent to their feelings in the most uncontrollable manner, which was fully reciprocated by the Reserves. One mistaken young man from Hudson, who took us for a member of the Railway club, in the exuberance of his joy, threw his arms around our neck, slapped our shoulders furiously, and committed other sacriligious [sic] acts, which we didn't feel like returning. The following is the

SCORE

FOREST CITY			RESERVE		
Players.	O.	R.	*Players*	O.	R
Smith, c.	7	1	Barrows, p.	4	4
Clark, 1b.	4	3	Hunker, c.	5	3
McEwen, 2b.	3	5	Hennan [sic], 2b.	3	5
Hurlburt, ss.	5	2	Smith, 1b.	4	5
Truesdale, rf.	4	2	Harvey, c.	4	4
Scates, lf.	3	3	Haskell, rf.	5	1
Stockley, p.	3	3	Brooks, 3b.	5	1
Gorham, cf.	2	5	Harrington, ss.	3	3
Brown, 3b.	5	3	Williams, lf.	4	3
Total	36	27	Total	37	27

INNINGS

	1st	2nd	3rd	4th	5th	6th	7th	8th	9th
Forest City	4	5	4	3	2	6	5	4	3 – 36
Reserves	0	7	2	4	3	2	6	5	8 – 37

Umpire, Samuel E. Williamson.
Scorers, A. P. Gerty, Forest City. ------- Reserve.
Time of game, 3 hours and 55 minutes.

The fielding of the Reserve Club was magnificent, while that of the Forest City was by no means up to their usual play. Two of their best players, Vilas and Hanna, were not in the game, their places being scarcely made good by Brown and Truesdale, of the second nine. Smith, who in the role of catcher is superb, played at a disadvantage, the felon [pus-producing infection] upon his hand, which disabled him at the time of the last game, being not entirely healed. He acted his part splendidly, however, notwithstanding. Of the play we cannot speak further, our space forbidding.

The conduct of the spectators was in general orderly and quiet; but we cannot pass without condemnation that of a knot of roughs, some of whom belonged to a club recently defeated by the Forest City, who repeatedly stopped balls which had passed the catcher of the Reserves. That this was not accidental is evidenced by the fact that none of the passed balls of the Forest City were interfered with. We are glad to know that the Hudson boys had no sympathy with this disgraceful unfairness, and condemned it heartily. [59]

After defeating the likes of Canton, Mansfield, the Hudson "Reserve," and other local clubs, the "Akrons" were ready for the big time. They scheduled a game with the powerful Forest City Club of Cleveland. In an item titled "Base Ball Excursion to Cleveland," the *Summit Beacon* enthusiastically notified its Base Ball readers that if they desired to witness the big game in Cleveland, then they should leave their names with E.A. Hooper at the train station as soon as possible. [60]

The *Summit Beacon* assured its readers that the game would be a top-notch contest: "Those who witness *that* game will undoubtedly see about as good playing as can be done with bat and ball, both clubs now being "monarchs" of all they have as yet "surveyed." [61]

The *Cleveland Morning Leader* concurred with the Akron newspaper in that it would be quite a contest, but it was more confident of the outcome.

Base Ball. – The match game between the Champions and the Akron Club will be played this afternoon [August 15] at 2 ½ o'clock at the grounds on Kinsman Street.

As before stated, this game is not for the prize bat and ball, but will nevertheless be an interesting one, and some fine playing will be witnessed. We feel perfectly serene of the results." [62]

The Cleveland *Morning Leader* provided extensive coverage of the big game. The report explained the "prize bat and ball" circumstances, described the uniforms of the Akron Club, painted a verbal picture of the Base Ball scene, analyzed the playing, showed the somewhat gloating attitude of the victors, and concluded with the statistics.

BASE BALL
Match Game Between the Forest City and Akron Clubs – The Former Victorious by a Score of 52 to 33.

...As stated, yesterday morning, the game was not for the prize ball and bat, the champions only being required to play for the custody of those, once in thirty days....

The Akron boys arrived by the morning train, buoyant with hopes of victory, and were received at the depot by a deputation of the Forest City. They are a fine-looking company of *athletes*, and made an attractive appearance in their neat and tasty uniform, consisting of white shirts and caps, red belts, and blue pantaloons with white cords *a la militaire*.

A goodly delegation of the citizens of Akron accompanied the Club to witness the play. An unabated interest on the part of Clevelanders was manifested in the game, and, as on previous occasions, a very large crowd collected upon the grounds. Until 4 o'clock the street cars went out heavily freighted, gay carriages thronged the streets, and hundreds wended their way thither on foot. The juvenile element of our population was, as usual, largely represented, from the homeless tatterdemalion to the well-dressed "young America" from Euclid Avenue.

The frequenters of base-ball matches cannot but note the increasing interest which is felt in this game by the fair sex. In the days of chivalry "ye ladyes fayre" were enthusiastic admirers of deeds of skill and daring, and were wont to crown the gallant knights of the tournament, and the victors of athletic games. This feeling seems to be hereditary in the daughters of Eve, and in the present generation, crops out in a passion for base ball. It is highly infectious and pervades all classes, the "*ton*" as well as the lowly. The ladies seem to have a full understanding of the game, and we noticed yesterday, several, attired in the height of fashion, seated in their carriages, with pencil and paper in hand, carefully "keeping tally," intently absorbed in the progress of the game. We shall expect to see lady scorers and umpires ere long introduced into our games.

[As for the game itself, the Forest City jumped into an early lead and never were threatened, especially after scoring 14 runs in the 4th inning. They steadily pulled away for a relatively easy victory over the "Akrons."]

The result was received with the usual acclamations by the crowd of spectators, although after the 4th inning they seemed to accept it as a foregone conclusion that the Akron boys would be defeated, and by no means as much interest was manifested as would have been had the contest been a closer one. Many of the members of the Akron club seemed to be disheartened, that the Fates were not more propitious, and their play was materially affected thereby. The play of the Forest City was not up to their usual standard, and neither party exhibited remarkable skill... The hitting of the Akron club was generally good, but their fielding was loose, and in this was their weakness. They saved ten "flys," however, to the Forest City's seven; but in passing the ball there was too much delay to be effective. Two of the first nine of the Forest City were not engaged – Hanna and Vilas – the former being absent on a trip to Lake Superior, and the latter having met with an accident which placed him *hors du baseball*, for the time. Their places were supplied by Brown and Truesdale of the second nine.

The Akron Club was hospitably entertained by the Forest City, at the Kinnard, at the close of the game, and left for home in the evening. The members of the Forest City speak in high terms of their courteous and gentlemanly opponents, and hope to meet them again in friendly strife, at some future time. While we have a natural pride in the success of our club, we extend to our visitors as much sympathy as can rationally be expected of us, under the circumstances...

FOREST CITY	R	O	AKRON	R	O
Smith, c.	7	2	Babcock, rf.	3	4
Clark, 1b.	7	3	Hudson, 1b.	3	5
McEwen, 2b.	8	1	Smith, 3b.	3	5

Hurlbut, ss...............	6	3	Hanford, F, ss............	4	2
Truesdale, 3b............	5	3	Hanford, Fred 2b........	5	1
Stockley, p...............	3	5	Hanscom, cf..............	3	3
Brown, rf.................	3	5	Buchtel, lf................	3	4
Gorham, lf...............	6	3	Angel, c...................	4	2
Scates, cf................	7	2	Rawson, p................	5	1
Total...............	52	27		33	27

[* It is important to note that the umpire was L. Brooks of the **Reserve** Club.] [63]

Although the "Akrons" received hospitable treatment from the Cleveland powerhouse, the representative of the "Akrons," who reported the game results to the *Summit Beacon*," was apparently somewhat distraught over the results of the game. On the way home, the "Akrons" passed through Hudson, and the sore-headed reporter didn't appreciate the reception that his team received there.

B. B. – "Akrons" vs. "Forest Citys."

The Match Game between the two veteran Clubs above named, came off as announced, in the city of Cleveland, on Thursday last – resulting in the defeat of the "Akrons," by a score of fifty-two to thirty-three. It was not so much the *good* playing of the "Forest Citys" as the unusually *poor* playing of the "Akrons" that conspired to bring about this result – it being conceded that the First Nine of the "Akrons" have never played so miserably since their organization – the only exceptions to the general rule being the Catcher [Angel, who scored four runs] and Second Baseman [Fred Hanford, who scored 5 times and only made one out]. The "Akrons" were entertained most courteously and hospitably by the "Forest Citys," though they complain of very shabby treatment by certain members of the "Reserves," and their admirers, on their arrival at the depot in Hudson, on their return home. [64]

The comment about the Hudson "Reserves" set in motion some of the first – if not the first – editorial letters regarding baseball. Someone in Hudson resented the remark that the "Reserves" of Hudson "shabbily treated" anyone; and he wanted his version of "Justice."

From Hudson – Vindication of the "Reserves."

Hudson, Aug. 26, 1867.

Ed. Beacon : Will you please, in justice to the "Reserves," correct the following statement, in your issue of the 22d inst., in the notice of the match game between the Akron and Forest City B. B. Clubs : -- "They (the Akrons) complained of being very shabbily treated by certain members of the "Reserves," and their admirers, on their arrival at the depot in Hudson, on their return home."

When the Akron Club returned home after their match with the "Forest Citys," there certainly was not more than one member of the Reserves in Hudson; and that gentleman, if in town, was not at the depot.

As to "being very shabbily treated" by any admirers of the "Reserves," we do not know what can be meant; unless umbrage was taken at the, perhaps, rather derisive cheering of a lot of rude boys who were loafing about the depot. But surely the actions of those "little shavers" should not be imputed to admirers of the Reserves!

After declining to accept a challenge from the Olympics of Hudson, probably at that time the second or third best B. B. Club in the county, without assigning any reason therefore, we should think the Akron Club would be loth [sic] to bring up the idea of shabby treatment in connection with any club in Hudson.

JUSTICE [65]

Another game between the Hudson "Reserves" and some Akronites was played on October 2nd. There was some argument concerning the roster of the Akron team, hence the term, "Akronites," was used above. The account of the game probably was not submitted to the *Summit Beacon*, but from the continuing feud between the teams' partisan letter-writers, which did appear in the above newspaper, one learns more than the results of the game.

Now, it was an Akronite's turn to give his version of "Justice." He probably signed his letter in such a way as to further irritate the correspondent from Hudson. The italics in the following letters are those of the letter writers.

That B B Report.

Akron, Oct. 12, 1867.

Ed. Beacon : I notice in the "Ball players Chronicle" of the 10th inst., an account of the game between a "Picked Nine" from this place and the Reserves of Hudson. The article says that the "Picked

Nine" were "from clubs in Akron, and other towns in Summit Counte [sic]." That is false, and whoever wrote the article *knew it at the time*. *Two* of the Nine were from Cuyahoga Falls, *regular* members of the Akron club. The play of the Reserves was rather *above* than *under* their usual standard, defeating the "Picked Nine" but seven tallies. Home runs and other different points of the game were omitted.

It was admitted by all present, including one or two of their own nine, that the "Muffins"* "did their level *best*," and would have done it *better*, had it not been for the most wretched one-sided umpiring; which was almost as bad as the umpiring at Cleveland between Forest City and Akron. It is an indisputable fact, that a nine, however sharp, cannot defeat both umpire and opponents. [*A muffin was a second-stringer or an unskilled player.]

"Justice." [66]

"Justice" of Akron had crossed the line of decency in attacking the umpires of Cleveland and Hudson. It took eleven days for the correspondent from Hudson to stew over Mr. "Justice's" remarks and to finalize his rebuttal. It was quite an epistle; and he was to have the final words in this feud concerning a "gentleman's game". Mr. "Reserve's" letter leads one to believe that the writer may have been a pre-law student at Western Reserve College.

"That B. B. Report."

Hudson, Oct. 23d, 1867.

Ed. Beacon: There appeared in the Beacon of the 17th inst., a communication severely criticizing, as unjust and untrue, the report published in the *Chronicle*, of a game of base ball, played at Akron, October 2nd. That there may be no misunderstanding I give you the report, as published in the *Chronicle*.

"A game was played Oct. 2d, at Akron, between the Reserve Club of Western Reserve College, and *an independent nine, picked from Clubs in Akron and other towns in Summit County. The play of the Reserves was rather below their usual standard,* yet there were some very pretty plays on both sides, a double play by Wheelock being especially noteworthy, he taking a hot ball from the bat at his base. – Hudson and Malone also made two nice double plays."

This was followed by a score, giving the number of outs, runs and bases on hits made by each man; also fly catches, foul bound catches, catches on strikes, base play, giving the number of men put

Ed **"Honest"** Searl, the umpire at Stan Hywet, proudly hoists his grandson and the team mascot of the Akron Black Sox, **Tommy** "Half Bounce" Searl. Tommy's father, Robert "One Bounce" **Searl** is the first baseman for the Sox.

out by each player, with the amount of assistance rendered, double plays, number of men out on fouls, and time of game.

The gentleman who signs himself "Justice" objects to the parts in italics, and complains that "home runs and other different points of the game were omitted."

In the first place, it was represented to the Reserves by *several* members of the nine that opposed them, that the Akron Club had broken up, but that a nine had been *selected* to play them at that time. The report does not say that the nine was the *best* that could be chosen. This nine was composed of gentlemen residing at Akron, Cuyahoga Falls, and Hudson, members of the Akron Club before its dissolution, with several members of the Summit Club, and a gentleman said to have been a member of a Club in Canton. They were entered as an "Independent Nine," as the "writer of the article" was informed by one of its members.

The gentleman also says that the "play of the Reserves was *above* their standard." Upon what ground does he make this assertion? Is he acquainted with the *statistical records* of the Reserves? Does he judge by their play at Hudson on June 29th, when one of their Nine, just from a bed of sickness, was physically unequal to his arduous task? Or does he judge from their play at Cleveland on July 26th, when they had not been together for 28 days?

In the *Chronicle* nothing was said about the play of the Picked Nine, because the writer was not sufficiently acquainted with their play to be able to judge. He *was* acquainted with the play of the Reserves. Their bad play was laid to the poor grounds, and what club could do itself justice there?

In regard to omissions, I would state the editor of the *Chronicle* refuses to publish what are called missed plays, as missed catches, wild throws, passed balls, &c. As for home runs, four were allowed by the umpire, whereas only three should have been allowed according to the rules, and they were not published on account of the difference in the scores.

Mr. Justice (?) concludes with some insulting cuts at the umpire. This needs no comment. Here, *if he did not before*, he descends from the dignity of a gentleman; for whenever a man implies that his integrity of character may be doubted, he is taking off much from his own cause.

RESERVE [67]

Although there was a game between the die-hard teams of Peninsula (43 runs) and Brecksville (25 runs) on November 14th, for all practical purposes the Base Ball season and "The Feud" came to an end on October 31st when a cold rain started at noon and turned into the first snow – " the 'feathery fluid' falling so thick and fast, that from six to ten inches covered the ground by ten o'clock." [68]

CHAPTER FIVE

THE ROSEWOOD BAT AND THE SILVER BALL

It had been six long years since the Ravenna Base Ball Club had made its first attempt to play Base Ball. Now, in mid-April of 1867 the club was revived, and the organization was eager to participate in the Base Ball fever that was sweeping the nation. The game was being touted as the "national pastime."

The *Portage County Democrat* highly endorsed the endeavors of the Ravenna Star Base Ball Club as well as the benefits of the game. The following article appeared in the newspaper on April 24, 1867.

Star Base Ball Club. – A number of the young men of Ravenna met on Friday evening last, and organized a Base Ball Club. The following officers were chosen: President, Robert B. Witter; Vice-Pres't, J. Henry Oakley; Secretary, M.H. Phillips; Treasurer, T.B. Alcorn; Directors, R.B. Witter, C. S. Cotter, E. B. Coolman.

The Club is conducted under the most approved rules controlling such organizations. The ground upon which the Club will hold its games has not been fully chosen, but it is quite probable that the County Fair Grounds will be the place selected. Base Ball is one of the most popular pastimes of the day, and involves science as well as muscular and athletic display. The Star Club now enrolls some twenty members, we believe, and an increase of membership is invited. Twenty or more young men should avail themselves of the opportunity afforded for healthful recreation and pleasure during the coming summer. [69]

Not all of the club's members were quite so young. Robert Witter, the president of the Star Club, was a 37-year old bachelor who was a harness-maker in Ravenna. Born in Nova Scotia, Witter had emigrated to Ravenna when he was twenty years old. He undoubtedly knew more about Base Ball as compared to the other members since he was elected the club's president and to the important position of team captain. The captaincy was equivalent to being team manager. [70]

John Henry Oakley, the Vice-President, was a 24-year old bachelor who had survived many fierce battles in the Civil War. He now operated a photographic gallery in Ravenna. He would become one of the team's scorers, and he would often play third base. [71]

Morton H. Phillips, the Secretary, was twenty years old. He had seen limited service in the army toward the end of the war. Phillips was a popular young man who knew how to play the infield. He would be the team's "Short Stop." [72]

Thomas B. Alcorn, the Treasurer, was only 18. His family was prominent in the community, and they resided at 525 East Main Street. [73]

Of the Directors, Charles S. Cotter was a 41-year old Civil War veteran. Prior to the war, he was the Captain of his own artillery battery. During the war, he rose to the rank of Colonel of the 1st Ohio Volunteer Light Artillery. Cotter had seen horrifying action in the western theater of the war. Cotter's business was now that of a "Gold-Silver-, & electroplater. Carriage plating a specialty." His role in the Star Club was primarily that of leadership, although he did try his hand at pitching on occasion. [74]

As for E. B. Coolman, the third director, he is somewhat of an enigma. "E. B." was probably related to Dewitt Clinton Coolman who was a leading financial figure and Democratic politician in the city. "E. Coolman" does not appear in the census reports or on any local cemetery records, but he does appear in the Star Club's line-up as their left fielder. [75]

With the high hopes that dwell in the springtime breasts of all ballplayers, the Ravenna Star Club gathered at the Driving Park on the Fair Grounds. Here they began to hone their skills and to learn the "science" of the game on every Tuesday, Thursday, and Saturday afternoons. The encouragement of the *Democrat* for the citizens to witness the practices was unnecessary because gentlemen, ladies, and children wandered out to the Fair Grounds out of curiosity to see this hotbed of Base Ball.

The Driving Park was only eight blocks east of the Courthouse and four blocks north on Freedom Street. A holiday atmosphere often prevailed there for political rallies, the county fair, a variety of horse races in the late summer, and now Base Ball.

In the early season, reports on the Ravenna Star usually appeared in the *Democrat's* "Local What-Not" column, which was a potpourri of local items printed in one or two sentences. On May 8, one "Local What-Not" was the announcement that "The Star Base Ball Club had its first game, at five o'clock Saturday afternoon, [May 4] at the Fair Ground." This was probably an intrasquad affair since no opponent was mentioned. It was not a balmy spring day in May because the "Local What-Not" also mentioned that "The freeze on Thursday night was severe, ice formed to the thickness of half an inch. Many are concerned for the safety of the earlier fruits." Nevertheless, the anticipation of spring was literally in the air since " During the past week the evening atmosphere has been decidedly smoky, caused by the burning of garden rubbish about town, preparatory to the making of the new gardens." [76]

The Star Club was still in need for players, presumably so that could have two complete teams for intrasquad games. Maybe they were looking for better talent also.

> The members of the "Star Base Ball Club" meet at their grounds at the Driving Park this (Wednesday) [May 8] evening for practice; and adjourn from there to the Engine house for a business meeting. We are informed that a few more members are wanted. [77]

On the 12th of June the *Democrat* announced that the Ravenna Star Club had been challenged to its first match game. The news item was sandwiched between two news briefs, which indicated that Base Ball had not yet reached its zenith in local interest. A man who fell from his horse and broke his left arm was equally important to Base Ball news. Following the Base Ball report, there was an item about a wandering urban cow that had been incarcerated in the new "Cow Pound." "The owner released his cow at an expense of $2.25, a sum that would have pastured it four or six weeks." Nevertheless:

> **Challenge.** – The first nine of the "Star Base Ball Club" have accepted a challenge from the first nine of Hudson to play a match game. The time selected is June 24 to come off at the Ravenna Driving Park. [78]

Judging by the *Democrat*'s report one week later, the excitement for the approaching opening game was beginning to escalate.

>**Base Ball Match**.— The Star Club of Ravenna, has accepted a challenge to play a match game with the Enterprise Club of Hudson. It has been arranged for the match to come off on Monday of next week – June 24 – at one o'clock p.m. at the Ravenna Driving Park. The match takes place between the first nine of each club. The "Enterprise" club was in practice last year, while the "first nine" of the Star Club were only chosen June 10th, so that the advantage of experience and practice would seem to be with the "Enterprise" boys. The following young gentlemen compose the first nine of the "Star Club" – and will hold the following positions in the match game:
>
>>J.B. Webber – Catcher.
>>O.J. Campbell – Pitcher.
>>M.H. Phillips – Short Stop.
>>I.J. Vance – 1st Base.
>>T.B. Alcorn – 2nd Base.
>>G.M. Phillips – 3rd Base.
>>E. Coolman – Left field.
>>R.B. Witter – Centerfield.
>>E. Swain – Right field.
>>J.H. Oakley – Scorer.
>
>The Driving Park will be open – free – to all who may desire to witness the sport on Monday afternoon next.[79]

The Hudson Enterprise was a formidable opponent for anyone, but they were especially challenging for the rookies of the Star Club. The Enterprise was one of the powerhouse teams in the area. They were experienced, and they were capable of scoring prolifically. The Ravenna Star had its work cut out for them.

On Monday afternoon the citizens of Ravenna and the visitors from Hudson thronged to the Fair Grounds to witness the Base Ball action. Captain Witter had fine-tuned his lineup by replacing G.M. Phillips with Wadsworth at third base.

The *Democrat* gave thorough coverage to the occasion, and its report tells the tale of the Star Club's Base Ball baptism.

Base Ball. – The match game between the "Enterprise" of Hudson and the "Star" club of Ravenna, took place at the Ravenna Driving Park Monday afternoon. The game continued for about three hours, and resulted in a victory for the "Enterprise" boys. The members of this club [the Enterprise] developed experience and strategic expertness, the fruit of two seasons devotion to the game. The Ravenna boys played a straight, square game, and played exceedingly well, for it must be remembered that their practice is of but little more than two week's duration. With a month's additional practice they can play the Enterprise a return match, and win with ease. At the conclusion of the match the two clubs partook of an elegant supper at the Gillette House, thus concluding the exercises of the occasion in the happiest manner. The "Enterprise" club was delighted with the courtesy of their hosts. The following is a summary of the innings.

ENTERPRISE		H.	L. R.	STAR		H.	L. R.
Reed,	C.	2	11	Webber,	C.	0	5
Seymour,	P.	1	10	Campbell,	P.	3	2
Bunnell,	S.S.	1	10	Phillips,	S.S.	3	2
F. Oviatt,	1B.	2	8	Vance,	1B.	4	2
J. Oviatt,	2B.	5	7	Alcorn,	2B.	3	3
M. Oviatt,	C.F.	2	10	Wadsworth,	3B.	2	3
A. Bishop,	3B.	4	7	Coolman,	L.F.	2	2
Star Jaqua,	R.F.	2	10	Swain,	R.F.	2	3
M. Moore,	L.F.	2	9	Witter,	C.F.	2	4
Total		21	82			21	26

[The first column represents the number of outs that were made.]

No. of innings played, 7. Time of game 3h 15m. Home Runs, J. Oviatt, 2 ; M. Oviatt, 1.

FLY CATCHES

ENTERPRISE		STAR	
Reed,	4	Webber,	2
Seymour,	1	Campbell,	2
		Alcorn,	2
		Wadsworth,	1
		Coolman,	1
TOTAL	5	TOTAL	8

Umpire – A.J. Mack, Western Reserve Club, Hudson.

Scorers – Enterprise Club, J.W. Holcomb.
Star " Jno. H. Oakley.
There was quite a large attendance of spectators at the Driving Park who enjoyed the sport with a keen relish. [80]

So, the home team lost by fifty-six runs in only seven innings. Nevertheless, the Star Club was not despondent. After all, didn't the reporter say that with a month's more practice the team would "win with ease" in a rematch?

The Star Club members were not cheapskates either. The Gillette House, where the Hudson boys were treated to a fine supper, was an excellent establishment on Main Street that had recently celebrated a one-year anniversary under the proprietorship of Col. R.A. Gillette.

> The Gillette House has now been open for a year, and its fame has been spread far and wide. Few hotels have succeeded in attaining and retaining so favorable and popular a position with the traveling public, and few indeed are so well worthy of that esteem. A good hotel is a letter of credit to town or city, and in the Gillette House, Ravenna enjoys a high superiority in this regard. [81]

The Star Club continued to practice three days a week at the Driving Park, and for a month they worked on the skills and strategy that were lacking in the game with the Enterprise Club. Part of the long delay between games is found in the *Democrat* of July 17th. It also shows the importance of R.B. Witter to the team.

> **Base Ball**. – Arrangements have been made for a friendly game of base ball between the second nines of the Mahoning Club of Warren and the Star of Ravenna, to come off Thursday or Friday of this week at the Driving Park; but Captain Witter of the "Star" having sprained his ankle badly, the game has been deferred until next week. [82]

The game was eventually slated for one o'clock on Thursday, July 25th. It was billed as a battle of second-teamers, also known as "muffins;" however, the Star Club had a sprinkling of its first nine in the line-up. Captain Witter's sprained ankle was still hurting him, so he moved from his outfield position to do the catching. Col. C. S. Cotter toed the pitching line. This battery would prove to be less effective than the Colonel's artillery battery on other fields. For the Ravenna Star there were 12 passed balls that day, which contributed to the nearly four-hour contest. The caliber of play is told in the statistics; however, the Mahoning Club was another of those experienced teams, even their second nine.

The Friendly Game of Base Ball, between the Mahoning Club of Warren, and the Star of Ravenna, took place on Thursday afternoon last [July 25th] at the Driving Park, and was attended by quite a crowd of people. The game was played by the second nines of each club, and resulted in the victory of the Mahoning Club. At the conclusion of the game the members of the two clubs sat down to an elegant supper at the Gillette, and the tournament was concluded in the happiest manner. The following is the score of the game:

MAHONING	R.	H.	L.	STAR.	R.	H.	L
Taylor, C.	11	2		Witter, C.	2	5	
Kinsman, 1b	11	1		Oakley, 1b.	3	3	
Howard, 2b.	8	4		Vance, 2b.	3	3	
Andrews, 3b.	9	4		Phillips, G. l.f.	4	3	
Fitch, s.s.	8	6		Phillips, M. s.s.	5	2	
Lauterman, p	11	2		Cotter, p.	4	3	
Hunt, r.f.	12	2		Ranney, 3b.	4	1	
Gray, l.f.	11	2		Gardiner, c.f.	2	1	
Hezlep, c.f.	10	4		Mason, r.f.	1	1	
Total	91	27			28	27	

FLY CATCHES

MAHONING		STAR	
Kinsman,	3	Oakley,	4
Howard,	1	Vance,	2
Andrews,	1	Phillips, G.	1
Lauterman,	1	Phillips, M.	1
Hezlep,	1	Cotter,	1
		Gardner,	1
Total	7	Total	10

FLYs MISSED

MAHONING 4　　　　STAR 7

HOME RUNS

MAHONING		STAR	0
Kinsman,	1		
Lauterman,	1		
Howard,	1		
Total	3		

PASSED BALLS

Taylor 6   Witter 12

UMPIRE – Ed. P. King. Scorers – Geo. F. Robinson, William R. Day. Time of game. 3h 45m.

After nearly two months, the Ravenna Star Club was ready for the return match with the Enterprise Club of Hudson. It was an opportunity to see if the Star Club could "win with ease" as the *Democrat* had predicted back in June, or at least see if they had improved.

The Enterprise made only two changes in their previous line-up – M. Oviatt was replaced by Blackman, and Moore was replaced by G. Bishop. On the other hand, the Star Club had made wholesale changes in preparation for the Enterprise boys. King would try his hand at pitching while Campbell moved to the outfield to replace Witter. Coolman shifted from left field to center. Butler replaced Webber at catcher. Alcorn moved from second to first base with Collins becoming the second sacker. Harris replaced Wadsworth at third base. With high hopes for this revised line-up, the Star Club boarded the train for Hudson.

Both the *Democrat* and the *Summit Beacon* of Akron covered the game. A new dimension was added to the *Democrat*'s Base Ball coverage. It not only reported the basic facts and statistics, but it also critiqued the action, all of which made for a complete and interesting account of the game for its readers.

Base Ball. – The first nine of the Ravenna Star Club, played a return match with the Enterprise Club of Hudson, on Saturday [August 10th] at the latter place. After a contest of four hours and a quarter, the Enterprise Club was the victor, the score standing 91 to 54.

SCORE

ENTERPRISE			STAR		
R.	H.L.		R.	H.L.	
Reed, c.	11	2	Swain, r.f.	8	1

Seymour, p.	9	5	Gardner, s.s.	2	5
Bishop,G. c.f.	12	3	King, p.	4	4
Bonnell, s.s.	13	0	Coolman,c.f.	6	4
Jaqua, r.f.	10	2	Alcorn, 1b.	6	4
Bishop,n.3b.	10	3	Butler, c.	9	1
Oviatt, J. 2b.	9	3	Harris, 3b.	9	1
Blackman,l.f.	9	4	Campbell, l.f.	8	1
Oviatt, F. 1b.	8	5	Collins. 2b.	2	6
	91	27		54	27

Flys Missed. -- Enterprise, 10 ; Star, 11.
Home Runs. – Enterprise. Seymour, 1, Reed, 1, Jaqua, 1, Bishop, A. 1, Blackman, 1.
Passed Balls – Butler, 16 ; Reed, 9.
Time of Game – 4 hours and 15 minutes. Umpire. – Prof. Barrows of Reserve Club.
Scorers. – Enterprise – W. Holcomb. Star – G.F Robinson, J. H. Oakley.
Runs Each Innings.–1 2 3 4 5 6 7 8 9
Enterprise. --   11 15 0 4 9 3 12 14 23
Star. --   6 3 7 4 6 6 10 1 11
[Author's note :The last two innings were horrendous for the Star Club, being outscored 37-12.]

COMMENTS

The wild throwing to bases of the Star was a noticeable feature in their play, resulting from a want of practice. The batting of the Enterprise throughout was excellent, five home runs being secured by them. The individual play in fly catches of Blackman, Coolman, and Campbell would win applause in any match. Blackman's one handed catch in the 6th innings was brilliant. [no glove] Bonnell's play at short stop was good. Gardner, at short stop evinced a tendency for capturing flys. King's pitching up to the 8th innings was swift and well directed; through the 8th and 9th, over exertion in the preceding innings showed plainly in his play. Enterprise having in their nine two good pitchers, by changing kept up an equality of pitching throughout. The Star nine would add much to their strength by having two good pitchers. [*Good starting pitching and a strong bullpen are still in demand today.*]The clubs were fortunate in securing an excellent umpire in Prof. Barrows of the Reserve club; his decisions were prompt and just, and very satisfactory. At the close of the game both clubs adjourned to the Mansion House, where an abundance of good things were awaiting the hungry "base ballers." After the feast, and an hour's stroll around the pleasant village of Hudson, the Club were conveyed to Ravenna on a through freight, arrangements having been made for their transportation early in the day. [84]

The Star Club was still winless, but they could be encouraged by their improved performance against the Enterprise Club. However, if there were any disgruntled players or spectators in the realm of the Star Club, a chance for redemption was in the offing. This golden (actually silver) opportunity was announced in the *Democrat* on August 21st.

> **Base Ball Prize At The County Fair.** – The Ladies of Ravenna have procured a Silver Ball and Rosewood Bat, which they offer, through the Star Club of Ravenna, as a prize to be competed for by all the Base Ball Clubs in the County, the prize game to be played on the second day of the County Fair. The Star Club is announcing the prize, also wish to say that it proposes only to play the winning club, provided three or more clubs enter into competition for the prize. All clubs intending to play for the Silver Ball and the Rosewood Bat, must notify M.H. Phillips, Secretary of the Star Club, Ravenna, by the 1st of September, that proper arrangements may be made, and a programme for the day issued. [85]

Things were looking up for the Star Club of Portage County. All they had to do for a little prestige was to watch the competition eliminate each other and then play one game for the prize. The odds were in their favor that they could win their own prize. Furthermore, the Enterprise Club was over in Summit County. A follow-up notice was printed the next week.

> It may be mentioned by way of diversity a Base Ball match will take place on the Wednesday, the second day of the Fair, for the prize of a silver Ball and a rosewood bat. There are many, it is presumed, that will feel an interest in witnessing a tournament of the kind. Let us appeal to the people of the County to give the matter attention, and put in our power to report for 1867 one of the most extensive and successful Fairs

ever held in this County. [86]

An interesting "Local What-Not" item regarding the prowess of the local nine appeared on the same day "The champion distance for throwing a ball is said to be three hundred and twelve feet. Some of the Ravenna players can nearly accomplish the feat."[87] [According to the last game report, their problem was not the length of their throws but their accuracy.]

A last chance for all of the Portage County teams to sign up for the Base Ball competition at the fair was issued on September 4th as the time for the county fair was fast approaching. The terms of the competition were apparently keeping teams from rushing to sign up.

To Base Ball Clubs

The Base Ball Clubs in the County are notified that their entering for competition for the Silver Ball and Rosewood Bat, at the County Fair, has been extended to Saturday, Sept. 7th, by which time all clubs desiring to compete for the prize must notify **M.H. Phillips**, Secretary, Ravenna. It is hoped that all the Base ball Clubs in the County will promptly enter their names for the contest. [88]

Excitement was in the air when the Portage County Fair opened on Wednesday, September 17. In recent years the fair had been plagued by cold rainy weather, but this day was very different: "...For once and a wonder the weather was delightful – blending, quite pleasantly, the brilliance of summer and the mellowness of the early autumn..." From all points of the compass, exhibitors and spectators in their horse-drawn buggies and wagons streamed along the dusty roads to the centralized county fair which drew them like a huge magnet. Eventually, a seemingly endless line of horses and vehicles parked around the perimeter of the grounds.

A loud cacophony of sounds arose amidst the busy scene as friends, relatives, and acquaintances hailed each other, children shrieked and scurried about, a variety of livestock added their vocalizations, and the numerous fowls on exhibit chattered and crowed.

Many of the fair-goers had a personal interest in the variety of exhibits. Among those things to be evaluated were the livestock, quilting and sewing items, baked and canned goods, farm produce of all kinds, and floral displays.

Then, there was the new attraction of Base Ball ! Only three teams had signed up for the grand prize of the Rosewood Bat and the Silver Ball; but for the Base Ball fans on this grand day, this meant nearly eight hours of action.

The first two Base Ball Clubs to face off against each other were named after their communities' geographical features. The Nelson Ledge was named for their large outcropping of bedrock, and the Kent Island was named for its playing area along the Cuyahoga River.

BASE BALL CONTEST

A very interesting and attractive feature of Wednesday was the Base Ball Contest for the prize of a Silver Ball and Rosewood Bat offered by the Ladies of Ravenna. Three Clubs – the **Ledge** of Nelson, **Island** of Kent, and **Star** of Ravenna were enlisted in the match, the programme being, first, a game between the **Ledge** and **Island** Clubs, the **Star** to play the winning club. The playground was encircled all day with a crowd of people and the amphitheatre of seats packed full of spectators. The presence of the friends of each club was manifested at times, as their favorites made "good hits." And so with the utmost good humor "the play" was conducted from 10 a.m. to 6 p.m.

THE FIRST GAME

The Islanders having won the toss, went to the field at 9:50 a.m. In the first innings the **LEDGE** boys scored three and the **ISLANDERS** nine tallies. This difference steadily increased until the close of the game, when the score stood, on even innings sixty-three to twenty-two, with two white-washes for the **Ledge** .... [The Ledge batted last in the ninth and scored five runs to give them a total of 27.]

Innings,	1	2	3	4	5	6	7	8	9	Total
Island,	9	10	5	5	6	3	11	8	11	63
Ledge,	3	2	0	8	5	3	0	1	5	27 .....

[Compared with its first nine back in August against the Hudson Enterprise Club, the Star Club had four new faces in the line-up, and on this day T. B. Alcorn toed the pitching line.

The Kent Island Club had one hour and fifty minutes from the end of its game against the Ledge to the start of the second game. They basically stayed with their line-up of the first game. Phillips was again the starting pitcher. Metlin replaced C. Ewell in right field.

[Otherwise, the line-up was the same by positions and batting order. The newspaper account continues.]

THE SECOND GAME,

Between the **STAR**, of Ravenna, and the winning nine, was called at 2:20 p.m., the Stars going to the field. At the close of the first inning the score stood four to four ; and the match promised to be a close one; but in the second innings the Islanders were whitewashed and the Star scored eight. In the fourth inning, Phillips, pitcher for the Island, gave out; and his place was taken by S. George, second base, who in return was relieved by Kent, called in. During the rest of the game the Stars gained without check, until at the end of the eighth inning the score stood : Star 79, Island 33 – the eighth being another whitewash for the Island – and the game was called, thus giving the ball and bat to the Stars.

The umpire, A.H. Hunker [who umped both games] of the Reserve club, was prompt and impartial in his decision; and gave entire satisfaction to all concerned....

	STAR			ISLAND	
	O.	R.		O.	R.
Butler, c.	0	11	Phillips, p.	2	2
Coolman, 1b.	5	5	George, H. c.	1	5
Alcorn, p.	4	8	Ewell, ss.	4	3
Collins, 2b.	1	11	Hepburn, 1b.	3	4
Oakley, 3b.	5	6	George, S., 2b.	3	2
Musson, ss.	2	10	Hoffman, 3b.	4	3
Webber, l.f.	1	12	Metlin, r.f.	2	3
Ney, r.f.	1	10	Boco, c.f.	3	4
Swain, c.f.	5	6	Classon, l.f.	1	5
			Kent, 2b.	1	2
Total	24	79		24	33

Innings,	1	2	3	4	5	6	7	8	Total
Star,	4	8	11	11	14	6	14	11	79
Island,	4	0	10	1	7	6	5	0	33

FLYS MISSED

Star – Collins, Musson 1 – total 3. Island – Phillips 2, H. George 1, Ewell 3, Hepburn 1, S. George 1, Boco 1, Classon 1 – Total 10.

HOME RUNS

Star – Collins 1, Webber 1 – total 2. Island – S. George 1, Metlin 1 – Total 2.

Passed balls --	Star 5,	Island 12.
Left on bases --	" 5	" 4.
Bases on called balls --	" 1	" 3.
Fouls struck --	" 34	" 15.
Out on fouls --	" 8	" 8.
Wild throws --	" 6	" 9.
Muffed balls --	" 5	" 8.

Time of game, 8h 40m [This is probably the total time for the tournament.]

A.H. Hunker, Umpire. Scorers, M.M. Sullivan, Island; M. Phillips, Star. [89]

One might say that the Star Club had taken the newspaper reporter's earlier advice to practice more, to minimize their wild throws, and to get better pitching. One could also argue that Kent's Island Club was tired after just playing a game, and then they had to face a fresh opponent. One could also say that this type of tournament was definitely favorable to the Star nine. Thus, the Kent Island Club immediately challenged the Ravenna Star to a rematch.

CHALLENGED. – The Star Base Ball Club, the winner of the silver ball and the rosewood bat at the county fair, are not to retain their championship unchallenged. The club retains the ball and bat for one year, and must play all comers in the county during that time. Any club winning the championship ball and bat must defeat the Star twice during the year. The Island Club, of Kent, are promptly after the victors at the county fair, and have challenged the Star boys. The challenge has been accepted, and the game will be played on the afternoon of Monday, October 7th, at the Ravenna Driving park. [90] [The game was later postponed to the 14th. The rules pertaining to the prize bat and ball also proved to be flexible.]

By October 9th, the game was billed as the "Base Ball match for the county championship." [91]

BASE BALL. – The second match between the Star Club of Ravenna, and the Island of Kent for the prize ball and bat, came off at the Driving Park, Monday afternoon, the 14th.

The game was called at half past two and continued into the dark, being called in the last half of the seventh inning – the "Island" having at that time only two men out, and the score standing Star 53, Island 40.

In the first inning the Star went to bat. The captain going out on three strikes, the Star began to lengthen their countenances; but by close playing they scored three to their opponents five. At the close of the second inning the score stood Island 10, Star 8. The third inning was more favorable to the Star; and resulted in a score of 13 for them and a "whitewash" for the Island. In the fourth inning the Star scored eight tallies, and the Island only one, but in the fifth with splendid batting on the Kent side, and weak pitching of the Stars, the Islanders made a run of fifteen to seven – thus gaining eight tallies, leaving them *only ten behind*. [Italics added.] At the close of the last even innings the score stood, Star 42, Island 31.

The playing of the Kent nine had improved very much since the Fair, their batting especially, being very fine. The batting of the Star compared very unfavorably with their usual play; many of the bats being "high flys."

The clubs parted with the best of feeling after taking supper at the Gillette. [There still had to be a nagging feeling among the Islanders that they had been had again. Their chances may have been slim, but they did score nine runs in the bottom of the seventh and were denied their final out.]

The gentlemanly umpire, Wheelock, of the Reserve Club, was strict, prompt and impartial, and gave satisfaction to both nine

STAR	R.	O.	ISLAND	R.	O.
Butler, c.	5	4	Phillips, p.	4	2
Ney, c.f.	7	0	H. George, s.s.	4	2
Musson, s.s.	7	0	Roland, c.	5	1
Coolman, 1b.	4	3	Boco, 1b.	6	0
Collins, 2b.	4	2	S. George, 2b.	3	3
Oakley, 3b.	2	3	Catlin, 3b.	2	3
Alcorn, p.	5	2	Stoffer, r.f.	2	3
Harris, l.f.	5	1	Ewell, c.	2	2
Leffingwell, r.f.	3	3	Richards, l.f.	3	2
Total	42	18		31	18

Innings,	1	2	3	4	5	6	Total
Star,	3	5	13	8	7	6	42
Island,	5	5	0	1	15	5	31

FLYS CAUGHT – Butler, Ney, Musson, Collman, and Alcorn, each 1; total 5. Island – Phillips 2, H. George 1, Roland 2, Catlin 2, Richards 1 ; total 8.

FLYS MISSED – Star 7. Island 10.

HOME RUNS – Island, Richards 2, Boco 1 – 3. Star, none.

FOULS STRUCK – Star 22, Island 13.

FOULS CAUGHT – Star 4, Island 1.

MISSED FOULS – Star 1, Island 1.

PASSED BALLS – Star 5, Island 14.

BASES ON CALLED BALLS – Star 3, Island 15.

LEFT ON BASES – Star 4, Island 2.

Time of game 3h 15m. [The game ended at 5:45. In mid-October it could very well have been dark.]

Umpire, C.F. Wheelock. Scorers, Sullivan, Island; Phillips, Star. [92]

The Ravenna Star Club could have rested on its laurels for the remainder of the year, but it chose to play another game.

Base Ball. – The Star Club of Ravenna have been challenged for the prize Bat and Ball and the County Championship by the Buckeye Club of Streetsboro. The challenge has been accepted and the game will be played at the Driving Park to-day (Wednesday) [October 23] commencing at 12:30 p.m. This is positively the last game to be played this season. [93]

At this point in the season, the Star Club may have been feeling a little over-confident. Maybe their sporting blood was up. Perhaps it was a matter of honor to accept the Buckeye's challenge. Maybe they just liked to play Base Ball. Whatever the reason, the Base Ball match with the Streetsboro Buckeye Club was one match too many for the Ravenna Star. They went down in an ignominious defeat. The coveted Rosewood Bat and Silver Ball prize, which the Ladies of Ravenna had purchased, was sadly relinquished to the Buckeye Club. The hometown reporter's disgust with the Star's horrendous play was obvious; yet his lament often had a comical touch to it.

This was the first time that such large print was used for a Base Ball article in the *Democrat*, so it was considered to be big news.

BASE BALL.
THE LAST MATCH OF THE SEASON
The Buckeyes Win the Championship Ball and Bat.
JUVENILE BASE BALL
Match Between Ravenna and Kent Clubs.
THE STAR JUNIORS WIN BY A SPLENDID SCORE.

The fourth match for the silver ball and rosewood bat came off between the "Buckeyes" of Streetsboro, and the "Stars" of Ravenna, at the Driving Park on last Wednesday afternoon. As the day was raw and chilly the number of spectators was considerably smaller than usual, and the Streetsboro element largely predominated. As the game progressed the few Ravennians present began to thin out and disappear, until at the close very few were left. A glance at the score will perhaps explain this strange lack of interest on their part.

The game was called at 1:10 p.m., the Stars taking the field. By the help of loose fielding the Buckeyes scored seven tallies, and retired to take the bat again after allowing the Stars to score only three. In the second inning the Buckeyes scored 11 and the Stars 13 tallies; thus leaving the Stars only two behind. The third inning did not prove so fortunate for the champions – the score standing at the close, Buckeyes 24, Stars 19. In the fourth inning Ravenna stock rapidly went down; and the friends of the Stars, who had hoped they would improve their play as the game advanced, began to despair. During this inning the Buckeyes scored 12, the Stars 4 tallies; the score standing 39 to 23 in favor of the Buckeyes. The next inning brought out a flash of good play from the Stars, which was quite reviving in its nature; but which was unfortunately as brief as it was brilliant. King took two foul balls in succession, and Alcorn touched his third man before reaching first; giving the Buckeyes a round 0 to grace their score with. After scoring six tallies, the champions retired, to be ignominiously whitewashed in the next two innings, during which the Buckeyes added 11 to their already large score. In the seventh, Musson, short stop of the Stars, was crippled in attempting to take a hot fly; and his place was taken by Ed. King, from the second nine. In the eighth and ninth the Buckeyes scored 13, Stars 9 tallies; the score standing at the close of the game 63 to 38.

The defeat of the Stars, and the consequent loss of the prize held by them, is attributable in part to the loss of Butler (who was unwell) behind the bat and the apparent indifference and carelessness of some of the Stars. King who was playing behind the bat for the first time, took fouls finely; but was unfortunate in throwing to bases – giving the Buckeyes a tally for nearly every throw. Some of the Stars appeared utterly unmindful of the trust confided in them by the ladies of the place, and amused themselves by dodging "hot liners" and turning their backs to the grounders to the disgust of the friends of both sides. The Buckeyes were good batters and fine runners and stole their second and third base with little difficulty.

As a matter of course the Stars have challenged the Buckeyes for another trial, which probably will not come off until next season. In the meantime the ladies can rest assured that the ball and bat are held by a nine who will take good care of them until they are obliged, as we hope they will be, to give them back to our now defeated Stars.

The two sides took supper at the Gillette House and parted with entire good feeling.

SCORE

BUCKEYES	O.	R.	STARS	O.	R.
Case, 1b.	2	7	Ney, c.f.	4	1
Wilcox, r.f.	5	5	Musson, s.s.	4	4
Peck, 3b.	3	8	Coolman, 1b.	4	4
Jenkins, s.s.	6	6	Collins, 2b.	2	6
Bently, c.	3	7	Alcorn, p.	2	4
Mellen, l.f.	2	8	Oakley, 3b.	5	2
McBain, c.f.	2	8	Harris, l.f.	3	5
Whitaker, 2b.	2	8	Leffingwell, r.f.	1	6
Stook, p.	2	6	King, c.	2	6

	Total	27	63				Total	27	38
Innings	1	2	3	4	5	6	7	8	9	Total
Buckeyes	7	11	9	12	0	10	1	9	4	63
Star	3	13	3	4	6	0	0	6	3	38

Home Runs – Bently 1, Collins 1 – 2.

Flys Caught – Buckeyes, Wilcox 1, Case 1, Jenkins 1, Bently 1, Whitaker 1, McBain 1 – 6. Stars – King 4, Leffingwell 1, Collins 1, Harris 1, Oakley 1, Coolman 1, -- 9.

Bases on Called Balls – Buckeyes 18, Stars 7. [Alcorn obviously had some control problems.]

Out on Fouls – Buckeyes 3, Stars 8.

Left on Bases – Buckeyes 5, Stars 7.

Passed Balls – Bently 2, King 5.

Time of game, 3h 20m.

Umpire – J.H. Seymour, Enterprise Club, Hudson.

Scorers – S.S. Crawford, G.M. Phillips. [94]

Yes, there is a life after Base Ball season. The "Local What-Not" items were varied on November 20th, 1867. A few real estate items appeared as some citizens were moving out of town, and others were moving in to take their places. For some untold reason a man jumped over a fence and severely dislocated his ankle. Butter, apples, quinces, and dressed pork were important enough to be mentioned. The town clock still was not very reliable at keeping accurate time. There was a fist fight at one of the depots: "The whiskey war-whoop was fiercely sounded, but no one was hurt..." "Thanksgiving comes on next week Thursday. It will be a day for big dinners and some drinking. No announcement of its formal observance has been made public here." [95]

The members of the Star Base Ball Club were back in their familiar haunts. The "boys" basked in the warmth of the iron stove in the fire station and enjoyed the fine cuisine at the Gillette House. A "Local What-Not" was reserved for them.

"The disabled base-ballers have now all recovered from their sprains, bruises, &c., and tell the story of their exploits with relish." [96]

80

CHAPTER SIX

UP AND AT 'EM AGAIN !

In late February 1868, the "base-ballers" hunched their bodies against the arctic blasts and blowing snow. Their destinations – the fire station, a grocery store, or a tavern – promised the warmth of a pot-bellied stove, the dreams of summer, and perhaps some heated conversation. The newcomers entered and quickly shut the door to minimize the wintry drafts, stomped the snow off their boots, and amid greetings and acknowledgments, made straight away to the stove to warm their hands. In the dimly lit room some of the boys leaned forward in their chairs; others hunkered on cracker barrels and wooden crates. As with many good conversations, it all began with, "What do you think of..."

The House of Representatives had just voted to impeach President Andrew Johnson for "high crimes and misdemeanors." The Ku Klux Klan was on a rampage in the South. Reconstruction of the states that had been in rebellion was a mess. Some of the prominent officers of the rebel army were back in political power in state governments; and for God's sake! some rebels were even heading back to the United States legislature. Some of the Union veterans in their midst wondered aloud, "Was all of the bloodshed and suffering done for naught?" Others allowed that, "If it weren't for the damned abolitionists and do-gooders, we wouldn't be in this mess. Now, what are we going to do about Base Ball this spring?"

By mid-April, affairs in Akron had acquired a rosier hue. The "base-ballers" gathered at E. A. Hooper's store at 129 Howard Street, where the proprietor advertised a new stock of elegant Meerschaum pipes, genuine Lone Star Tobacco, a full supply of Durham Smoking Tobacco direct from Wilmington, N. C., and those new "self-igniting cigars." The *Summit Beacon*'s editor seemed as eager about Base Ball as the gentlemen who gathered at Hooper's store.

Base Ball

The annual meeting of the Base Ball Club took place last

Herrick and Cannon stocked Base Ball shoes presumably in their toy department at 122 South Howard St. (Note the two hobby horses protruding from the second story window.) Just up the street and on the opposite corner was E. A. Hooper's tobacco shop, which was in back of the Empire House, a fine hotel and dining establishment. Photo: Courtesy of the University of Akron Archives.

evening at E. A. Hooper's store. The following is the list of officers elected for the ensuing year.

President – G. T. Perkins
Vice president – Dr. Ashmun
Secretary – W. A. Palmer
Treasurer – E. A. Hooper
Directors – E. B. Rawson, C. R. Howe, W. C. Babcock.

The times for general practice are Tuesday and Friday afternoons of each week, at 3 o'clock P. M. Set the ball rolling and look out for muffins and hope for no broken bones and broken noses. We promise lively times in this interesting game this summer.[97]

E. A. Hooper's business neighbors were cashing in on the Base Ball fever that spring; they may have been Akron's first sporting goods stores. Herrick and Cannon's on North Howard advertised "Base Balls, Bats, and Croquet Clubs" at wholesale prices. The *Beacon* also noted, "Base Ball Shoes at New York Boot and Shoe Store, 106 Howard St." [98]

Thirty-four miles east at Warren, the editor of the *Western Reserve Chronicle* had lost his enthusiasm for Base Ball that spring. The sport was obviously thriving in Trumbull County, but Mr. Editor was having no part of it. Knowing his politics, he probably was upset over the results of the Johnson impeachment trial before the Senate. In May, the final score was 35-19 for conviction. That would have been a good Base Ball score, but a two-thirds majority was required in the Senate; so old "My Policy" (Johnson) escaped with a one-vote victory. Mr. Editor was also appalled at the number of injuries in the 1867 season; and he may have been one of the first editors to decry the over-emphasis of Base Ball. His editorial was a damning denunciation of what he had previously called the "National Pastime."

Base Ball.

Through our exchanges we notice that in many places the base ball mania is setting in again, with all the vigor of last season, when, to many minds it was over-done. That the game was carried to excess none will deny. Then nearly everybody had "base ball on the brain," and many of the players had it on their fingers, in their eyes and mouths, and elsewhere, as numerous fractures would attest. A base ballist was not unfrequently a base-bawler, and one who come [sic] off the field without a few teeth loosened, a black eye, sore head, or a finger or so dislocated, was a mere tyro – no player at all; but the one who could manage to get both arms in a sling and his head in a bandage as the result of a "spirited game," was the lion of the day – a hero. At prominent matches, the attendance of physicians was no uncommon thing, and nearly as much a matter of course as at duels, their services being considerably more likely to be needed than at duels of the latter day sort. Between missiles used – base ball and pistol ball – it is an open question as to which was the most dangerous. If the game was played for amusement and exercise, the balls were unnecessarily hard, and in one or two instances that we remember, fatal* injuries were sustained, while there are many young men who are more or less crippled for life in the too harsh exercises. Among other tests, a most foolish custom prevailed of rating a player's proficiency according to the hardness of the ball he could catch and hold. To such an extent was this carried, that so far as the chance for injury was concerned, one might about as well have played with "brickbats," with the advantage in favor of the latter, they being the easiest to dodge.

The game of base ball, played within bounds, is deservedly popular as a healthful, muscle-developing amusement; but, played as it was last season, it was not only an injurious but dangerous sport, the exercises taken being altogether too harsh and violent.

The young men of Warren, at present, do not seem disposed to risk their anatomies in the game this summer, but if they should conclude to revive it, we trust it will be produced in a modified form, with less lengthy reports of their match games for publication.[99] [The author did not see any articles in his research concerning any player being killed in a baseball game at that time; but that is not to say that it never happened.]

Back in Akron, the ballists were enjoying the fine spring weather in which the strawberry crop promised to be the best in years. By late June the Akron and Hudson boys were at it again. Once more, the Reserve Club was a formidable opponent.

HUDSON

Hudson, June 29, 1868.
Dear Beacon: The first of a series of match games between

the Akrons and the Reserve Club, was played on Saturday, June 27th, on the Reserve's grounds. The Akrons were on hand early and the game began near two o'clock, the Akrons taking the field. And batting of the Reserves was very good, but the outside playing was better, and it was the opposite character of the Akrons. Their best playing was shown on the inside; but we would recommend to them that carefulness on bases is a very good element in a club. Several fine flies were caught on both sides. MALONE [A] caught two fine fouls near first base, while HERRINGTON [R] succeeded in capturing the same number at his position [c], one of which was exceedingly difficult, therefore a fine catch. LEHMAN [A, 2b] took in a high fly in good style while running toward first base. SHEETS [A, lf] also did well, receiving a long one from the bat of CURTIS, and throwing it to second base. CURTIS [R, lf] made two good catches and several excellent throws; at one time putting a man out at third. The shortstop of each club [Hanford (R) and Pierong (A)] took in a good fly apiece; and their throwing also was worthy of admiration. SMITH [R, 1b] took three difficult flys near first base, and LATIMER [R, 2b] a high one near second. I give the score.

[In the box score and statistics section, the reader had to figure the score for himself. The Reserve won handily, 49-31. Beach (3b) had seven hits, and Smith scored eight runs to lead the Reserve attack. As always, the Hudson writer added a non-Base Ball item.]

The Baccalaureate sermon yesterday was preached by Prof. Cutler, and was very fine indeed. The sermon before the Missionary Association in the evening, was also very fine and was preached by Mr. Page, of Warren. More next week.

NEMO [100]

Judging from the absence of news print, the rivalry between the Akron Club and the Reserves of Hudson never attained the level of heated competition that they created in the previous season. "Nemo" penned another lengthy letter to the *Beacon* in mid-September; and there was only one paragraph about Base Ball, perhaps due to a Hudson loss.

The "Enterprise" came back, the other day, rather chopfallen from the defeat they received from the Akron Club. But they have elected some new players into their nine, and have determined to try it again. They speak with great praise of the superior playing of the Akron Club, and especially that of their new Catcher. [NEMO did not mention the score of the game.] [101]

The previously mentioned game may have been part of the Base Ball extravaganza that was conducted at the Richfield Fair. Six clubs were represented: Akron, Enterprise, Medina, Granger, Brecksville, and Peninsula. In a four-inning contest, the Akrons defeated the Enterprise 15-13. Medina defeated Granger 37-33 in five innings. Then the Brecksville nine got on a roll. They routed Peninsula 36-13 in 4 ½ innings, edged Medina 8-7 in only three innings, and outscored Akron 9-5 in just a two-inning affair. The first prize of $20 was awarded to the Brecksville Club; and the Akrons garnered the $10 for second place. [102]

One of the Base Ball highlights in the summer of '68 occurred when the Mutual Club of East Liberty, Pennsylvania (four miles east of downtown Pittsburgh) boarded the train and headed west to barnstorm through some Ohio towns. After playing the Ravenna Star Club on Friday, August 21, the Mutuals entrained for Akron to play a game on the following day.

In the previous week, the Akrons had "a trial" with their neighborhood rival, the Middlebury Club, in which the Akrons prevailed 47-42. In touting the coming attraction – Mutuals vs Akron – the *Summit Beacon* anticipated a quality match: "Both being thoroughly trained clubs, some good playing may be looked for." [103]

The enthusiasts in the Akron area were not disappointed. The large crowd appreciated the numerous defensive gems, which made for a relatively low score and short game. The game reporter's perceptions and descriptions painted a mental picture of this fine August afternoon of Base Ball.

> **B. B. – Akrons vs Mutuals.** – The match game of Base Ball between the Akron Club and the Mutuals, of Pittsburgh, Pa., came off according to announcement, on Saturday last, resulting in favor of the Akrons by a score of 21-11.
>
> The pitcher and first baseman of the Mutuals are splendid players; the remainder of the club only medium. RAWSON as pitcher of the Akrons, was grand, taking a "hot ball" direct from the bat, coming with the velocity from a Parrot gun.* -- MALONE, as first baseman, took everything that came to

him, with one exception, which was not his fault. SHEETS "gobbled" some handsome "flys," which was applauded loud and long by the 2000 spectators in attendance. The Mutuals were whitewashed four times, and the Akrons twice. We give the score:

AKRONS	O.	R.	MUTUALS	O.	R.
Hanford, 2b	2	2	Haven, p	4	0
Pierong, ss	5	1	Lyle, c	3	1
Mack, c	4	2	Tomer, 1b	4	0
Babcock, 3b	5	2	J. McKelvy, 2b	2	2
Scott, lf	3	3	Martin, lf	4	2
Malone, 1b	3	2	Myers, rf	2	3
Rawson, p	1	4	N. McKelvy, ss	3	2
Sheets, cf	2	3	Wormcastle, 3b	2	0
Funk, rf	2	2	S. McKelvy, cf	2	1
	27	21		27	11

INNINGS.

	1	2	3	4	5	6	7	8	9	
Akrons –	1	3	4	2	5	3	0	3	0 –	21
Mutuals –	0	1	1	5	3	0	0	0	1 –	11

Time of Game – 2 hours, 25 minutes.
Umpire – R. McNulty, Mutual B.B. Club, Pittsburgh.
Scorers – W. Baird, W. F. Aul. [104]

[* A Parrot gun was a common type of Civil War cannon.]

The Warren *Chronicle* may have suppressed a variety of Base Ball games by refusing to print or to minimize game reports, but the *Summit Beacon* reveled in the National Pastime whether it involved a fancy club or an industrial nine. In the summer of '68, a host of "Grant Boys in Blue" organizations touted Gen. U. S. Grant in the upcoming presidential election. One such group formed at Akron's prominent Buckeye Mower and Reaper Works. The *Beacon* proclaimed, "It will do good service in 'mowing' down the copperheads and 'raking' in the Union voters at the coming election." The company also furnished two teams, the "Molders" and the "Finishers," for an intra-company game in which "The Molders were 'sent to grass' by a score of 45 to 32." Not to be outdone, the wood workmen and the blacksmiths of Messrs. Collins, Bell, & Co.'s carriage establishment in Akron played a muffin game in which the wood workmen carved out a 25-16 victory. The flourishing pottery trade was represented when the Akron Potters traveled to nearby Mogadore to challenge their Potters. The Mogadore tradesmen won 18-16 without some punster commenting about something "going to pot." Besides the entertainment and competitive values of these games, they furnished free advertising for their companies. [105]

The real "Boys in Blue," who had experienced severe combat just 3 ½ years previously, were now hurling less deadly missiles.

The Military Game. – The match game of base ball between the nines of the 104th O.V.I. and the 6th Ohio Battery, came off, as announced, last Thursday afternoon, resulting in the defeat of the Battery boys by a score of 59-32. The rain did not discourage the "veteran" players in the least, though a few of both nines were about "used up."

We are requested to tender the thanks of the players to Mr. E. A. Hooper, for his splendid umpiring of the game; to the Akron B. B. Club, for the use of their grounds and "utensils," and to Capt. A. P. Baldwin, for the luxuries served up for the occasion.

Since the above was written, we understand the 104th boys have received a challenge from the Union Club of Morrisiana, N. Y., the champions of the United States. At an informal meeting of the 104th ['s] nine a day or two ago, the matter was under consideration, but nothing definite was determined upon. The feeling seemed to be in favor of wasting no more strength and science on second class material. Another meeting will be held in a few days at Blain's Cross Roads, when the question will be finally settled. [106]

Oddly named teams were sure to catch the editor's eye. The "Alpines" of Wadsworth (certainly not a mountainous community) lost to the Akron "Resolutes" 66-46 in a 4 ½ hour contest. The "Old Persimmons" of Tallmadge were thumped twice by the Middlebury Unions," (a common name), 76-22 and 89-25. [107]

However, the oddest teams in the summer of '68 were chosen for their body *weight*; and judging by the amount of print these teams received, they played the grandest game of the summer. For enthusiasm, entertainment, and humor, the game between the "Fats" and "Leans" could not be outdone. As for performances in this five-inning affair, one must judge for himself.

FATS VS LEANS
The Great Base Ball "Tournament."

One of the most novel and exciting games of base ball came off in this city on Tuesday afternoon, ever before witnessed here or elsewhere. "Leans and Fats," in other places have met "bat to bat" before, it is true; but we will venture to say that never before was there so much genuine fun evolved in so brief a period this side of the Celestial Empire, as resulted from the challenging of the "Leans" by the "Fats" of this city, as announced in the following poster and programme:

GRAND MATCH GAME!
BASE BALL!
LEANS VS FATS!
WIND AGAINST BOTTOM!
Tuesday, July 28th, 1868, at 3 o'clock P.M.

Lean Nine	Fat Nine
E. A. Hooper, c, 121 lbs.	N. W. Goodhue, c, 225 lbs.
C. Johnston, ss, 96 ½ lbs.	R. F. Hoor, ss, 224 lbs.
H. McKinney, 2b, 135 lbs.	H. P. Hitchcock, 2b, 210 lbs.
J. N. Baldwin, lf, 134 lbs.	W. H. Payne, lf, 225 lbs.
J. Koch, rf, 100 lbs.	Milton Moore, rf, 230 lbs.
M. T. Cutter, p, 145 lbs.	Geo. Weimer, p, 205 lbs.
H. E. Abbey, 1b, 145 lbs.	B. Bosworth, 1b, 225 lbs.
W. K. Ingersoll, 3b, 123 lbs.	H. I. Carr, 3b, 216 lbs.
J. A. Sumner, cf, 134 lbs.	J. J. Hall, cf, 215 lbs.
Scorer – J. D. Buchtel	Scorer – W. B. Raymond
Surgeon – W. C. Jacobs	Surgeon – T. McEbright

Umpire – W. G. Robinson; "Orator of the Day," Gen. A. C. Voris; Sutler, George Washington Martin; Ambulance Driver, Eber Hawkins; Marshal, Charles brown; Ass't Marshal, A. G. Shields.

GRAND PROCESSION!
The procession will form at 2 o'clock, P.M., in front of W. G. Robinson's News Depot, in the following order:
1. Marshals (on Mules.) 2. First National (Colored) Band. 3. Ambulance and "Medicine" chest. 4. Orator, (in regimentals.) 5. Scorers, Surgeons, Umpire, Reporters, &c. 6. Summit Cornet Band. 7. Fat Nine, single file, six feet apart. 8. Marble's Band. 9. Lean Nine, twelve feet apart. 10. Sutler's wagon. 11. Fire department, in charge

of Supt. J. C. McNeil. 12. Mayor and City Council, in charge of City marshal Butler. 13. Benevolent Societies. 14. Akron B.B. Club, Buckeye B.B. Club, Resolute B.B. Club, Central Grant Club, Young Men's Democratic Club, and such other "Clubs" as will be necessary to enforce order, in charge of Assistant Marshal Parker. 15. Citizens in carriages. 16. Citizens on foot. 17. Everybody fond of fun.

The procession will march down Howard Street to market, up Market to Prospect to Grace park, and form in a hollow square, or square hollow, (immaterial which) around the ground, in order to prevent the chilly July breezes from visiting the heads, (particularly the Fats,) too roughly during the progress of the game.

THERE WILL BE ROOM FOR ALL !
By Order of the Committee:

Long before the time appointed for the formation of the procession our streets were crowded with people, and every conceivable species of conveyance, from the common one-horse dray and express wagon, to the splendid four-horse barouche. Punctually at the time, the Marshals appeared, with their "mules," magnificently comparisoned and themselves duly booted and spurred, and commenced the herculean task of forming the immense mass of vehicles, quadrupeds and bipeds present into a procession. The National "Sable" Band led off in gallant style, and the programme was followed as nearly as possible, the benevolent societies of the city being represented by the Liedertafels [a long time Akron German society], who were each and all gotten up *a la comique*, expressly for the occasion. The Summit Cornet and marble's Band occupied the places assigned to them in the procession, and did their full share of "blowing" while en route to the "field of battle."

Owing to the torridity of the atmosphere, it was deemed inadvisable to subject the distinguished com-bat-ants [sic] to the fatigues of so liquefactious a march, and they were consequently packed upon drays – the "Fats" two to a dray, and the "Leans" all upon one – on which they were safely hauled to the grounds. The ambulances, (Bonstedt's ice wagons,) and the sutler's and commissary wagons, (the various express wagons of the city,) were all duly freighted and the procession proper of vehicles alone, reached from the corner of Howard Street nearly to the Park, while "straggling" carriages, equestrians and pedestrians, completely filled the streets and sidewalks the entire distance.

It is estimated that there was from 2500 to 3000 persons upon the grounds during the progress of the game, which was entered into with great spirit by both parties, the fats going first to bat. It is impossible of course, within the limits of this brief report, to give anything like an adequate description of the game and the numerous good "points" made by the several players. The fats led off well, and though gradually distanced as the game progressed, all showed remarkably good *bottom* to the last, while the leans, though "blowing" a good deal over their victory, were apparently in as good "wind" at the close as at the beginning of the game. The following is the official score of the game:

LEANS	O.	R.	FATS	O.	R.
Hooper, c.	1	5	Goodhue, ss.	2	3
Johnson, ss.	0	6	Hoor, c	3	2
McKinney, 2b	0	6	Hitchcock, 2b	4	1
Baldwin, lf	2	4	Payne, lf	1	4
Koch, rf	1	5	Moore, rf	1	3
Cutter, p	3	3	Weimer, p	1	3
Abbey, 1b	2	4	Bosworth, 1b	1	3
Ingersoll, 3b	4	2	Carr, 3b	2	2
Sumner, cf	2	2	Hall, cf	0	2
	15	37		15	22

INNINGS

	1	2	3	4	5	
Leans	14	14	4	2	3	– 37
Fats	6	4	0	7	5	– 22.

Home Runs – Hooper 1, Payne 1, Carr 1
Fly Catches – Hitchcock 1
Missed Flys – Johnson 1, Goodhue 1, Bosworth 1, Carr 1.
Umpire – W. G. Robinson
Scorers – W. B. Raymond, J. D. Buchtel.

The Surgeons were faithful in the discharge of their duties, and it is probably owing to their frequent use of the *sponge* that we are enabled to still quote *tallow* and *lard* "firm" and "steady". At the close of the game, the several prizes which had been prepared, were duly presented by the "Orator of the day," as follows: Mammoth ball and bat (ball 6 ½ inches in diameter, and bat 4 ¾ feet long) to the winning club; Bottle of Mrs. Winslow's Soothing Syrup for the best score, to H. McKINNEY; Box Chewing Gum for best batting, to H. L. CARR; Stick Cabler Candy for most home runs, divided between,

HOOPER, CARR, and PAYNE; mammoth Picture Book for most fly catches (one) to HITCHCOCK.

A collection was taken up on the ground to aid in defraying the expenses of the entertainment, amounting to $15.28, and everybody went home satisfied that however it may be with the "national game," in general, as a "time and money killer," they had been well paid for their attendance upon the fat and lean contest between wind and bottom. [108]

The Leans went on to play the City Fathers in a pair of "muffin games" that August; but the town's enthusiasm and the press' coverage was a pittance compared to that of the Fats versus the Leans. In effect, the sequels were much like twice-warmed-over hash, which is fine if one is a true hash lover.

> **The Result.** – The muffin game between the City Fathers and the leans came off as per announcement, on Friday last, the game of seven innings being one of the most closely contested of any during the season, the official nines taking and keeping the lead until the last inning, when the Leans came up with and distanced them by two tallies, the score standing at the close, Leans 22, Council 20. We were promised the official score, but it has failed to come to hand. The defeated party – plucky to the last – immediately challenged the victors to a full game of nine innings, which was promptly accepted …
> **B. B.** – Game number two between the Leans and the City Fathers, which came off on Friday afternoon last, resulted as did the first, in favor of the Leans by a score of 52-46. [109]

Of particular interest in the original Fats versus Leans extravaganza was the participation of Akron's African Americans. All of the newspapers cited in this chapter had been ardent anti-slavery and pro-Union organs; but the *Summit Beacon* was foremost in announcing news of their "colored" population, although the minimal coverage was probably due to the small number of African Americans in the city. As noted in the game report, "The National 'Sable' Band led [the parade] off in gallant style." The band also advertised in the 1868 Akron Business Directory: "First National Cornet Band – Colored – Brass Instruments – 15 persons – Charles Brown,

Leader."[110]

In mid-August the *Beacon* proudly noted the political persuasion of the black residents – they too advocated the election of U.S. Grant – and their celebration of an extremely important event that occurred six years previously.

> The colored voters of this city, about one hundred in number, formed a Grant Club at their hall in Hanscom's block, on Monday evening. The "First National Band" furnished music for the occasion...
>
> The colored people of this city are making preparations to celebrate the anniversary of the Emancipation Proclamation by President Lincoln, on the 22nd day of September.[111]

Although their numbers were small, one would think that this vibrant and dynamic group of citizens would sponsor a Base Ball club. After all, the national "Championship of the colored clubs" was played in 1867 with the Brooklyn "Uniques" defeating the visiting Philadelphia "Excelsiors," 37-24.[112] The National Pastime was a long way from being integrated, but segregation did not prevent the courageous and skilled young black people from enjoying the magnificent game of Base Ball. Only *one* brief mention of a "colored" match game indicated that the area's African Americans were involved in the grand old game. The old Akron-Hudson rivalry took on a new dimension in August, 1868.

> Base Ball. – A match game of Base Ball was played on Monday last, between the colored Independents, of Hudson, and the Second Nationals, of Akron, resulting in favor of the Independents by a score of 61-29.[113]

The Akron Black Sox Strike a Classic Pose at Hale Farm and Village.

CHAPTER SEVEN

WHERE HAVE ALL THE TROPHIES GONE?

Lyman W. Hall, the straightforward editor of the *Portage County Democrat*, was a political animal first and secondly a Base Ball enthusiast. In spite of its title, the *Democrat* was an unabashed advocate of the Republican Party. Thus, Lyman and his son and partner, Halsey, were highly incensed when President Andrew Johnson escaped removal from office. The Halls spared no vituperation in lambasting the turncoat Republican senators who voted not guilty. However, the Ravenna publishers laid aside their mourning and denunciations when the serious presidential campaigning began in the late summer of 1868. Sandwiched between these political events was the Base Ball news of the local nine.

As for the Ravenna Star Club, who happened to be primarily Democrats, the chief thought was how to win back the Rosewood Bat and the Silver Ball from that pesky Streetsboro nine. The Star Club's quest was tantamount to a crusade, because it also involved regaining the unqualified respect of the local ladies who had purchased the prize ball and bat.

BASE BALL. – A return match between the Star Club of Ravenna and the Buckeye Club of Streetsboro on Tuesday, June 30th for the championship of the County and the prize rosewood bat and silver ball. It will be an interesting occasion. The prize bat and ball are now held by the Buckeye Club. [114]

The headlines trumpeted the results of the fantastic return match of the Stars versus the Buckeyes. June 30th, 1868 would go down in Ravenna Star history as a day of glory.

BASE BALL.
Champion Match – Buckeyes vs. Stars.

STARS WIN BY A SINGLE TALLY.

The return match between the Buckeye Club of Streetsboro and the Star Club of Ravenna, for the Rosewood Bat and the Silver Ball, came off at Streetsboro, Tuesday June 30th.

This prize, it will be remembered, was won from the Stars by the Buckeye Club last fall, the latter beating the Star Club more than 20 runs. The weather on Tuesday, though rainy during the early part of the day, cleared up beautifully, being everything that could be desired at the time [the] game was called. About 10 o'clock, everything being in readiness, play was commenced; the Stars having won the choice went to the field, the Buckeyes at the bat started with a [first inning] score of 1 to 8 for the Stars. To the wild throwing of the Buckeyes in this and subsequent innings, more than to anything else, can be attributed to their defeat.

At the end of the third inning, so rapidly had the Stars increased their lead that the score then stood 15 to 5 in their favor; in the next four innings the Buckeyes succeeded in scoring 29 to 16 for their opponents, giving them a lead of three runs, and having got over the nervousness evinced in the first part of the game were playing much steadier. In the next two innings the Stars added 10 to 6 for the Buckeyes, giving them the victory by a single tally. Owing to its closeness the game was a very exciting one, which was quite evident from the continuous and not very discriminate cheering of the crowd in attendance. Of individual play on the part of the Stars, the fielding of Wadsworth was excellent. He caught two beautiful flys, one in the second and one in the sixth inning. Butler behind the bat was superb, throwing to the bases with a precision and swiftness seldom exceeded. Webber, Somerville and Swain played well in their positions. Somerville, changed to left field in the 5th inning, made the best catch of the game, taking a "sky scraper" from Wicks' bat. Ney and Webber at the bat both made several strong hits. Ney, in the 9th inning making the best bat of the game. On the part of the Buckeye Club, Jenkins at short stop was hard to beat, taking several flys in fine style while on the keen run. Peck and Mellen did good execution at bat, both being swift runners and strong strikers, the former making the only home run of the game. Both Clubs have several weak points which practice would better very much. It seems to us it might be well for the Buckeyes to select a ground a little less hilly, or provide step ladders for the fielders. At the close of the game both Clubs sat down to an elegant "spread" given by the Buckeye Club. We understand a return game will be played soon; also that several clubs in the county are anxious for a chance at the Bat and Ball.

We append the score.

STARS	R.	O.	BUCKEYES	R.	O.
Webber, lf	8	1	Mellen, lf	7	2
Butler, c	5	4	Case, 1b	6	2
Ney, 2b	4	3	Foot, c	4	4
Swain, p	3	4	Bentley, 3b	5	2
Wadsworth, cf	2	3	Humphrey, 2b	2	4
Somerville, 3b	2	4	Wicks, p	3	4
Gardner, ss	5	4	Wilcox, cf	4	2
Campbell, rf	7	1	Peck, rf	5	3
Oakley, 1b	5	3	Jenkins, ss	4	4
Total	41	27	Total	40	27

INNINGS

	1	2	3	4	5	6	7	8	9	Total
Buckeye	1	1	3	2	12	9	6	2	4	40
Star	8	1	6	4	5	5	2	7	3	41

FLY CATCHES

Webber 1, Butler 3, Swain 1, Wadsworth 2, Somerville 2, Gardner 1, Oakley 2 – total for Stars 12.

Humphrey 1, Wicks 1, Jenkins 2, Wilcox 1 – total for Buckeyes, 5.

FLYS MISSED – Buckeyes 11, Stars 2.
FOULS STRUCK – Buckeyes 11, Stars 22.
HOME RUNS – Buckeyes 1.
BASES ON CALLED BALLS – Buckeyes 4, Stars 6.
PASSED BALLS – Buckeyes 4, Stars 4.
UMPIRE – J. W. Holcomb, Enterprise Club, Hudson.
SCORERS – Buckeyes, S. S. Crawford; Stars, M. H. Phillips.
Time of game, 3 hours, 25 minutes. [115]

Judging from the lack of press coverage, Base Ball enthusiasm took a month and half hiatus in Ravenna; but in mid-August the fever struck the town again. The "Mutuals" of Pittsburgh were coming to town, and the upstart Hiram "Boanerges" were challenging for possession of the coveted Rosewood Bat and the Silver Ball. Due to the Mutuals' traveling expenses, the spectators were being assessed a gate fee; but the game was free for the Boanerges contest. The two games received top billing in the *Democrat*.

BASE BALL
TWO MATCH GAMES
Stars of Ravenna and Mutuals of East Liberty, Pa.
Championship of the County, The Silver Ball and Rosewood Bat.
Stars of Ravenna vs. Boanerges of Hiram.

Two match games of Base Ball are to take place at the Fair Ground this week; one, on Friday, and one on Saturday. The STAR Club of Ravenna having accepted a challenge from the MUTUALS of East Liberty, Pa., have named Friday next, August 21st, as the day on which to play the friendly game. The MUTUALS are reported to be fine players and are making a short tour to meet in friendly contest a number of local clubs in this region of country. The STARS are in excellent practice, and will give a good account of themselves on the field. This club has designated as its chosen nine the following players: ...[At this point, the only change from the previous lineup was that E. P. Hatfield was to replace Campbell.]

This game will be one of interest, and it is presumed will be watched by a large audience, especially as it is the first public game played here this season, [An explanation for the hiatus?] and affords an opportunity to witness the performance of a well disciplined club from abroad. To defray some expenses, necessarily incurred, a gate fee of Fifteen cents will be charged. The game will be called at precisely 1 P.M. Let the day and its amusement be remembered.

CHAMPION GAME.

Upon Saturday, the STAR Club will meet the BOANERGES of Hiram in contest for the championship of the County, the prize silver ball and rosewood bat. This game will, of course, be exciting and lively, and will be likely to attract quite an attendance from out of town. The Hiram Club is in good playing practice and has won some laurels this season in its home vicinity. The game on Saturday will be called at 1 P.M. The entrance to the Fair grounds on Saturday will be free.[116]

Except for being pounded 12-0 in the third inning and 16-3 in the ninth, the Star Club put up a good scrap against the barnstorming visitors from Pittsburgh. However, after the post-game banquet, the Mutuals moved on to Akron with a 53-32 victory under their belts also.

The amazing thing about the Boanerges-Star report was that every at-bat was printed in the *Democrat*. In this era of Base Ball, it was the only time that the *Democrat* did this; and no other newspaper, except the Cleveland *Leader*, came close to such complete coverage of a Base Ball match.

BASE BALL.
Stars of Ravenna and Mutuals of East Liberty, Pa.
THE MUTUALS THE WINNERS.
Championship of the County. The Silver Ball and Rosewood Bat.
Stars of Ravenna vs. Boanerges of Hiram.
THE STARS THE WINNERS.

The game between the Mutuals of East Liberty,Pa., and the Stars of Ravenna, came off as was advertised, on the grounds of the latter Club on Friday August 21st, 1868.

[The] game was called at five minutes past two. The Stars having won the toss, took the field the field and sent their opponents to bat.

The score on the first two innings shows close playing upon both sides, the game at this time standing 8 to 5 in favor of the Mutuals. The third inning was to say the least, not favorable to the Stars, they being whitewashed, while the Mutuals scored 12 runs. The end of the 7th inning saw the whitewashes even, and the Stars with their friends quite elated. In the ninth inning the Mutuals seemed to bend to their work with renewed vigor, and aided by some loose fielding upon the part of the Stars, succeeded in scoring 16 runs which brought their total to 53.

They took the field determined if possible to add one more to the Star list of whitewashes, but in this they were disappointed, for the Stars by careful work closed the game with an addition of 3 runs to their score bringing the total to 32.

Several instances of individual play are worthy of note.

Haven, the pitcher of the Mutuals sent in some "hot one" and this swift pitching worked rather more to their own disadvantage than otherwise. For the reason that their catcher is not with them and they had not a man in their 9 who could stop Haven's balls [sic]. [Author's note: With the advent of faster pitches, one can see where the game is progressing into a pitcher's game, rather than a batter's game in which the pitch is lobbed across the plate.] W. F. McKelvey played well at short stop, while Tomer, the "half breed" as he was facetiously called, did splendid execution at 1st Base.

Of the Stars, Butler, behind the bat, was, as usual, superb, having only three passed balls during the game. Coolman did well at R.F., 2d B, and P. In fact, he seems peculiarly adapted to every position on the nine. Oakley slaughtered many at 1st. Somerville at 3d B. labored under serious inconvenience in consequence of a tree which stood almost directly in his way and kept him from taking several flies.

The Batting was mostly so low that the fielders had but little to do. But what they did do was well done; especially by Webber in left field. The Umpire, Mr. Hanford, gave general satisfaction and showed by his decisions that he knew whereof he affirmed.

After the game, the Clubs repaired to the Exchange where they found a bountiful repast awaiting them to which they did ample justice. The Mutuals are a set of jovial boys, and everything passed off pleasantly. From here they went to try their skill with the Akron boys. [See the previous chapter for the Mutuals vs. Akron.]

MUTUALS	R.	O.	STARS	R.	O.
B. Haven, p.	7	3	Webber, lf.	3	4
H.T. Lyle, c.	7	3	Butler, c.	6	0
Jno. Martin, lf.	8	1	Ney, 2b.	2	4
W.P. Aull, cf.	4	5	Swain, p.	4	4
Jno. McKelvey, 2b.	6	3	Wadsworth, cf.	3	2
-- Tomer, 1b.	3	6	Somerville, 3b.	3	4
W.F. McKelvey, s.s.	7	1	Gardner, s.s.	5	2
S.W. Castle, 3b.	4	2	Coolman, rf.	3	3
S.M. McKelvey, rf.	7	3	Oakley, 1b.	3	4
Total	53	27	Total	32	27

RUNS ON EACH INNINGS.

	1	2	3	4	5	6	7	8	9	Total
MUTUALS	4	4	12	2	4	2	0	9	16	53
STARS	2	3	0	9	4	2	1	8	3	32

Flies caught – Mutuals 6, Stars 5.
Flies missed – Mutuals 5, Stars 2.
Passed balls – Mutuals 17, Stars 3.
Time of game, 3 hours and 10 minutes.
Umpire, F. H. Hanford, of the Reserve Club, Hudson.
Scorers – Mutuals, Wm. Myers; Stars, M. H. Phillips.

The first game between the Boanerges of Hiram and the Stars of Ravenna, for the County ball and Bat, came off on Saturday last, the 22d inst., on the Driving Park at Ravenna, and was witnessed by a goodly crowd of people, who seemed highly interested in our national game, cheering and jeering, as suited their humor, over the good or bad work of the players, and venturing not a little currency on the result of the game. Somebody or something stirred up considerable ill-feeling among the lookers on, but did not succeed in greatly disturbing the equanimity of the two Nines, who throughout the entire game displayed the best feeling, setting an example that might well have been followed by their friends on the outside.

Play was called at 10 minutes before 2 o'clock, and Boanerges took the bat.

[An extensive play-by-play report followed. Some of the highlights are given here.]

...3 balls called let Webber (R) to 1st base [obviously a difference to the modern-day base on balls] ...Wadsworth (R) out on splendid fly taken by Squire in left field...Pow (H) sent a grounder to right field, and by aid of wild throws of Stars, cleared the bases, and brought in 4 tallies...Dudley (H) out on splendid fly taken by Webber, who sent the ball to Coolman, running out Ewalt. Good double play...Coolman (R) stole home in face of pitcher and catcher with ball in their hands; home run by Oakley...

STARS	R.	O.	BOANERGES	R.	O.
Webber, lf.	8	2	Proctor, c.	8	0
Butler, c.	9	0	Farr, p	7	3
Ney, rf.	4	5	Wilcox, L., s.s.	3	3
Swain, p.	5	3	Wilcox, J., 1b	6	2
Wadsworth, cf.	4	4	Pow, 2b	4	3
Somerville, 3b	6	3	Ewalt, 3b	3	3
Gardner, s.s.	3	4	Squire, lf	3	4
Coolman, 2b	5	2	Dudley, cf	3	3
Oakley, 1b	5	4	Rodifer, rf	3	6

[Total] 40 47   [Total] 49 27
TOTAL RUNS EACH INNINGS.

	1	2	3	4	5	6	7	8	9	Total
Boanergers	1	3	3	12	1	1	2	15	2	40
Stars	7	1	0	6	11	11	9	2	2	49

Flies caught – Boanergers – Proctor 1, Wilcox L. 1, Wilcox J 3, Ewalt 1, Squier 1, total 7. Stars – Webber 2, Butler 5, Swain 1, Wadsworth 2, Gardner 3, Coolman 1, Oakley 1, total 15.

Flies missed – Boanerges – Farr 1, L. Wilcox 1, J. Wilcox 2, Squier 1, Total 5. Stars – Webber 1, Ney 1, Wadsworth 1, Gardner 2, Total 5.

Passed balls – Butler 4; Proctor 7.

Fouls struck – Boanergers – Proctor 2, L. Wilcox 1, Dudley 4, Rodifer 5, Total 12. Stars – Butler 10, Swain 3, Ney 2, Somerville 4, Gardner 10, Oakley 1, Total 30.

Home runs – Boanergers – Farr 1, Rodifer 1 – Total 2. Stars – Webber 1, Oakley 1 – Total 2.

Bases on called balls – Boanergers 7, Stars 2.

Time of game, 3h 50m.

Umpire – F. A. Hanford, Western Reserve B.B.C.

Scorers – Boanergers, W. U. Masters; Stars, M. H. Phillips.

Mr. Hanford, of Cuyahoga Falls, umpired the game throughout in a satisfactory manner, giving his decisions promptly, doing his duty as fairly as it is possible for any umpire. Good feeling prevailed throughout between the two nines, and the Boanergers went home well satisfied with the courteous treatment they had received. The game was close, and the Stars must not expect that this victory will insure them another over the same club. [117]

The spectators, who attended the county championship game, and others of a later age must have wondered what a Boanerger was and why the Hiram boys chose to be called the Boanerges Club. Webster's Dictionary offers several possible answers. If the college boys viewed themselves as "sons of wrath," they chose the Aramaic derivation of the word. However, the Greek derivation of the word may have sounded less threatening and appeared more sporting for heavy hitters – "sons of thunder." The first definition of Boanerges states that it was a term that Jesus used for the Apostles John and James. The college boys, who were well known for their orating powers, debating abilities, and ministerial aspirations, may have chosen Webster's second definition of Boanerges. After all, Hiram's best known orator, professor, Civil War general, United States Representative, and minister of the gospel was none other than James A. Garfield, who was destined to be the 20th President of the United States. Definition 2 reads, "a loudmouthed vociferous preacher or orator."

After such thorough coverage of the Boanergers vs Stars game, the *Democrat*'s inkwell suddenly and mysteriously went dry for the original Ravenna Star Base Ball Club. The Stars' last hurrah briefly appeared in the *Democrat's* first weekly edition of September.

> BASE BALL. – Upon Saturday last the Star Juniors of Ravenna played a friendly game with the Hiram Base Ball Club. The Star Juniors were successful in a score of 42 to 12.
>
> Upon Monday [September 7] a return match for the Silver Ball and Rosewood bat was played between the Stars of Ravenna and the Buckeyes of Streetsboro. The game was played at the Fair Grounds, Ravenna. – The Buckeyes were victorious by a score of 35 to 30. [118]

The Hiram Student's August edition reported that it was the Hiram Jockey Club that lost to the Star Juniors by 46 to 12. The newspaper also noted the Stars' loss to the Buckeyes and that the Boanergers were itching for another chance at the coveted Rosewood Bat and Silver Ball. In the meantime, there "was a friendly game by the Boanerges with the Welshfield club played Monday, Sep. 7th, resulting favorably to Hiram, the score standing 98 to 38." [119]

The last words for the Boanerges of 1868 appeared in the *Hiram Student*'s October Edition.

> BASE BALL. – The "Boanerges" of Hiram have played during the month only two match games, in both of which they were victorious.
>
> Sept. 30th, the game played with the "Lightfoots" at Chardon resulted, in eight innings, in a score of 52-19.
>
> Oct. 12th, the match was on the College grounds with the "Eureka" club of Cleveland. Result – Boanerges 55, Eureka 22.
>
> Quite a large number of spectators were on the ground to wit-

> ness the latter game, including students of both sexes and citizens of the town. Some very fine playing attracted attention, wherein the participants won much commendation and displayed fine physical training. [120]

Although there was no evidence of complaining letters to the editor, one wonders if the Ravenna editor had a change of heart akin to that of the Warren *Chronicle's* editor. Did he feel that he had over-emphasized a frivolous pursuit at the expense of more important news? As for the demise of the original Star Club, logical explanations can be partially substantiated. Some members of the Star Club moved out of town for better employment, while others headed off to college to study for various professions. Wedding bells and family responsibilities also played a part in breaking up the old gang. Still, the promising Star Juniors could have filled the depleted ranks, but there is no evidence of that ever happening. Over the next few years, brief notices about the Star Junior Base Ball Club occasionally surfaced, but eventually they too completely disappeared.

An important Ravenna news item in July 1869 was the visit of Jesse R. Grant and wife, the father and mother of the President of the United States. Jesse, who had operated a tannery in Ravenna prior to relocating at Point Pleasant, Ohio, were guests of Col. William Frazer and E. P. Brainard, Esq. In the same column of items, the Star Juniors were allotted two small notices; and their press coverage never got any better.

> The Star Junior Base Ball Club of Ravenna and the Buckeye Club of Cleveland played a match game at the Ravenna Fair Grounds on Tuesday. The ages of the players are from fifteen to twenty years. [No score was given.] ...
>
> The Star Junior Base Ball Club of Ravenna met the Olympics of Hudson, at the latter place on Saturday, for a friendly game. The score stood Olympics 24: Star Juniors 15. It is proper to state that the Star Juniors are a younger class of players than the Olympics, and had the disadvantage of a twelve mile ride in the rain before the game. [121]

Although *Beadle's Dime Base Ball Player* condemned professionalism in the sport; in some quarters professional Base Ball began to dominate the newspaper coverage of the National Pastime.

In the spring of '69, the Cleveland Forest City Club decided to go "big time;" and their first move was to bring in a "ringer" to do their pitching. The Cleveland *Leader*, which apparently thought that the new Cleveland nine was the next best thing to the invention of bread, extolled the new acquisition.

> **THE NEW PITCHER.** – A. G. Pratt, the new pitcher for the Forest City base ball club, has arrived in this city. A practice game was played yesterday [May 10th] and Mr. Pratt showed himself fully entitled to the reputation which has preceded him. His delivery of the ball is swift and almost unerring and he will contribute not a little to the laurels we expect to be won by this club during the season. [122]

The college clubs and local nines no longer stood a chance against the powerful Cleveland team. The Hudson Reserves, who had wrested the prize bat and ball from the Forest City in 1867, were thoroughly manhandled by a 75-17 score. The Hiram Boanerges fared better in losing 20-5 to the Cleveland powerhouse. Some of the *Leader's* pithy comments on the latter game illustrated that the days of lobbing the ball over the plate were gone; and furthermore, it was open season for criticizing the umpire.

> ...The Forest Club, as usual, fielded closely and well. Pratt, Ward, Allison, and Johnson, all, in fact, playing a careful, pretty game. The Boaberges caught well and threw indifferently, but were utterly at sea before the swift pitching of Pratt. Their judgment at times showed their wont of practice with sharp playing clubs, but on the whole their game was far from being a poor one.
>
> Of the umpire we should feel disinclined to speak were it not that some comment is necessary to a correct appreciation of the game. We readily acquit him of any intention to be unfair, but that he was totally incompetent the veriest *gamin* in the crowd knew before the second inning was finished. He seemed incapable of distinguishing a swift ball from a wildly pitched one, and in the course of the game he gave the Boanerges six bases on called balls, and their opponents none, while the pitching of Pratt was perfection with that of Bickel [of Hiram]. The latter, though he sent the balls in

wildly, had a very effective way of altering their speed and worrying a striker, so that the Forest City men, although trying hard, could never get a lead on him... [123]

Down state, an all-professional Base Ball dynasty had been created in what one biased Cleveland writer referred to as "Porkopolis," a reference to Cincinnati's meat packing industry. Regardless of jaundiced and perhaps jealous northern opinions, the Red Stockings' fans were in love with their team, the first "Red Machine."

Cincinnati is wild over the triumphs of her Red Stockings. Crowds besiege the telegraph and newspaper offices every evening, bulletin boards are put up about town to announce the result of games, and the *Commercial*, which prints solid columns of telegraph reports of their contests, is reaping a perfect harvest of scrip. [124]

Twice in the previous season, the Red Stockings handily defeated the Lake Erie team by the scores of 44-22 and 33-14. However, with the addition of their new pitcher and improved play, the Forest City nine entertained notions of becoming one of the elite teams in the nation. Their only obstacle was the Ohio River team on June 2nd, and the *Leader* excitedly anticipated the match-up.

BASE BALL – THE GREAT MATCH TODAY. – It will be hardly necessary to remind our readers that to-day brings with it the match game of base ball between the famous Cincinnati Club and the Forest City nine, an event which will prove a worthy and auspicious opening of the ball season of '69. The overwhelming victory of the "Red Stockings" at Mansfield yesterday confirms all that has been said about the condition of the nine. Made up of the finest base ball material that the country can supply, and trained by two months of daily practice, the nine of the Cincinnati Club is to-day perhaps the most perfectly disciplined organization of its kind ever seen in this country. There is no weakness, no mediocrity anywhere, but pitcher, catcher, basemen and fieldmen work together like a finely adjusted machine...

Both clubs are certainly far stronger than when they met last season, and the contest to-day between the two leading teams of Ohio will be an event of no secondary interest. The personal relation between the two clubs is of the most cordial character, and whatever may be the result of the game, the glory will be in a certain sense "all in the family." Tickets of admission are for sale at Rawson's book store and at the entrance gates of the grounds. Visitors will take the Kinsman street or Garden street cars, both of which run near the grounds. Policemen will be in attendance to look after horses and carriages left outside the enclosure. If the day should prove propitious the occasion will doubtless call out one of the largest crowds ever seen at a match game in this city. Play will begin precisely at three o'clock. [125]

The battle of Ohio's Base Ball titans occurred on a beautiful spring day near the shores of Lake Erie. Indeed, "the attendance of spectators was large, the *elite* of the city being well represented.."

BASE BALL.
The Game Between the Forest City and "Red Stockings" – The Latter Victorious by a Score of 25-6.

The base ball campaign for the season was fairly inaugurated on Wednesday by the long anticipated game between the Forest City club and the famous "Red Stockings" of Cincinnati. The latter club has just started on its eastern tour, the first game of the series having been played with the Independents of Mansfield on Tuesday. The high degree of proficiency attained by the Porkopolis boys had been heralded in advance of their coming, and all expected one of the finest games ever witnessed in this city. In this none were disappointed, although there were some among us who fondly hugged the elusive idea that our own club – the terror of all base ballers in northern Ohio – had a faint idea of the rudiments of the game, and it was generally believed that our boys would be able to hold the "Red Stockings" pretty "level." There were some blank faces, therefore, when it was known that our boys had been beaten by the cheerful score of 25 to 6.

…. The Red Stockings are a splendid company of athletes and their courteous and gentlemanly bearing, no less than their skillful play, at bat and in field, won them hosts of friends. Their batting was but little superior to that of the Forest City, but their fielding was superb. They seemed to have a way of harvesting inflies [sic], grounders and every other kind of ball, that was never excelled by any club that has visited our city. So like clockwork did they play together that it seemed as each was but part of a perfect machine. From the furthest part of the field the ball was thrown with the force of a catapult and with almost unerring precision, while the in-fielders shot the ball to the bases with an accuracy that betokened certain death to those who were striving for the sand-bags... [126]

As the shadows lengthened in the ninth inning on that warm spring day, many of the Cleveland spectators may have reluctantly admitted the following ratio: Red Stockings are to Forest City as Forest City is to Boanerges. Nevertheless, these professional teams exhibited such an amazing physical prowess and strategic knowledge of the game, especially when compared to the local crossroads, political, industrial, or urban neighborhood nines. In the eyes of the avid spectators and the newspaper reporters, the magnificent professionals burst upon the Base Ball scene like super novas; and in the process the lesser teams were reduced to mere twinkles.

As the old Base Ball Clubs faded away in the annals of time, one wonders what ever happened to the prize bats and balls. Were they left outdoors in a weedy field to disintegrate from exposure to rain, snow, frost, or a blazing sun? Were they deposited in some dusty and forgotten shed, garage, barn, or attic? Were they the victims of overly tidy mothers who threw the treasured items out of the house, those forerunners of the mothers who threw away Junior's baseball cards? Whatever did happen to the Rosewood Bat and the Silver Ball?

CHAPTER EIGHT

AN EPITAPH FOR THE STAR CLUB

Some concept of the Base Ball skills, courage, and enthusiasm of the Ravenna Stars and their contemporaries has been revealed. Yet, how did they play the game of life after their ball playing days were over; and for what would they be remembered after they played life's final inning? Now, some people contend that sports participation builds character, while others contend that it merely reveals what character already exists. Either way, herein lies a glimpse of the character of some of the Star Club members and the varied paths that they traveled.

Robert B. Witter, the captain of the Ravenna Star Base ball Club, was born in Truro, Nova Scotia on October 29, 1829. Bob's father died in 1848, and a year later the 20-year old Witter emigrated to the United States. Bob's mother, two sisters, and a brother moved to Portage County in 1850. In 1854 Bob settled in Ravenna where he plied his trade as a harness-maker until 1863. Thereafter, he operated a livery stable in the city. During the Civil War, Witter did not serve in the military; however, he and many other businessmen in the town raised funds and supplies for the boys in blue. In 1868 Witter was appointed the Street Commissioner of Ravenna.

In October 1872, around Bob's 43rd birthday, he ended his long bachelorhood by marrying the young widow of Dr. Charles G. Steadman. Bob and Mary Witter had one daughter, Mary A. Marital life for Witter lasted only 6 ½ years; Mary died on May 30, 1879.

Bob Witter surely had a zest for life. Besides playing Base Ball at the age of 38, he and a partner operated an ice skating rink on the Ravenna square. In addition, Bob must have been a patient, enduring fellow, especially in May 1876 when the following news items appeared in the *Democrat*.

Last week Friday, the remains of the late Dr. C. G. Stedman, with the monument erected to his memory, were, by direction of his widow – now Mrs. R. B. Witter, of Ravenna – removed from the Randolph cemetery and placed in a burial lot in the Ravenna cemetery.... [Mary was interred next to her first husband in 1879; and Bob was laid to rest at her other side 14 years later.]

About three o'clock, Tuesday afternoon, as Mr. R. B. Witter was exercising a pair of colts, the team became frightened and wheeled about short, at the north-east corner of main and Chestnut streets, upset the carriage and smashed it up. Mr. Witter suffered the dislocation of an ankle in his struggle with the excited horses.

When Bob Witter died on May 9, 1893 at the age of 64, impressive services were conducted at the Congregational Church, which he regularly attended. The *Democrat* wrote a lengthy obituary titled "The Farewell Tribute." Two former teammates contributed in the farewell to Bob Witter; John Henry Oakley sang in the quartet and Hon. D. C. Coolman served as a pallbearer. The final rite was not an uplifting experience for the survivors. The Rev. S. W. Meek referred to Bob Witter as a "dreadful sufferer" and an "afflicted invalid." Rev. Meek also added the following to the lament.

> ...he [Rev. Meek] spoke of the frequent changes of habitation that fell to his [Witter's] lot, and of the sorrow of a broken home circle which came to sadden his days, experiences that burdened him with more than the ordinary trials and vicissitudes of human experience. He had for years been weighted with the responsibilities of harassing business cares, and knew more of the struggles, battles and hardships of life than fell to the lot of many...
>
> Life, said the speaker, is a battle. We come into the world the most imperfect of all the animal creation. So frail and fragile is the tender infant hold on life that two out of every three die in early childhood. Where the vitality endures to riper years, the survivors find manifold other troubles to perplex and worry them...
>
> Life is trouble. Life is a battle. "You ask why this is so? I answer candidly that I cannot tell, and know of no one who can. We know that those who have burdens to bear and crosses to endure, and take them up cheerfully and willingly

are the ones who grow into the large wide, rich and noble manhood...

Amidst the gloom and doom on this spring day, one can imagine the old-timers ambling out the front door of the church and into the rays of the sun. Surely, one of them remembered that shining and exciting summer when Bob Witter was a Base Ball player and the Captain of his team. [127]

John Henry Oakley, who excelled at first base and catcher for the Ravenna Stars, was allotted the full amount of exciting innings in the game of life. Oakley was born On December 9, 1842 in Charlestown Township, but he and his three sisters were raised in Ravenna. When John died on Valentines Day, 1919, his passing made front page news in the *Ravenna Republican*. In between his natal day and his demise, John's life appeared to be a blessing to those around him.

> J. H. Oakley passed into rest at his home ... after eight years of failing health, terminating in an illness that confined him to his bed since last August...
> Mr. Oakley spent all of his seventy-six years as a citizen of his native Portage County, in which he was widely known as a soldier, photographer and postmaster at Ravenna, and highly esteemed in all circles. It is a story of sound American citizenship, large business experiences, fine social qualities and friendly relations with his fellow men for whom he had a never failing word of cheer and a kindly greeting, memories of which will endure with those who knew and admired this estimable trait of character, and who appreciated the superior qualities that stamped him a man of taste and refinement. In all of his relations he so lived that it may be truly said of him, "Well done, good and faithful servant."...
> At the beginning of the War of the Rebellion Mr. Oakley was one of the first to respond to the call for volunteers, and enlisted on April 25, 1861, for three months' service in Company G, 7th Ohio Volunteer Infantry with which he served until August of that year. On October 15 of the same year he re-enlisted for three years in Battery I, First Ohio Light Artillery, better known as "Leather Breeches Battery,"

with which he served until December 10, 1864, when he was honorably discharged by reason of expiration of his term of enlistment...

[Oakley witnessed some of the fiercest action in the Army of the Potomac from Second Bull Run through Gettysburg. Battery I was then transferred to the western theater of the war, where it blasted its cannons from the Battle of Chattanooga to the doors of Atlanta.]

After his discharge Mr. Oakley returned to Ravenna where he opened a photographic gallery, in which business he continued until May, 1898; when he was appointed postmaster of Ravenna by President McKinley, and re-appointed by President Roosevelt in 1902, and again in 1906.

During his administration, which covered a period of thirteen years, the first city and rural carrier service was installed through his efforts...

[On June 19, 1872, Oakley married Isodene E. Horr, whose family was among the early settlers. At a time when families were large, John and Isodene had only two sons. Being an enthusiastic Fraternal man, who included the G.A.R. among his eight memberships, might partially explain the smaller family.]

The story of his life would be very incomplete without mention of his absorbing love of music and of his accomplishments as singer and instrumental player. He had a tenor voice of rare range and purity, and sang for many years in church choirs and other local organizations, including the famed Philharmonic Society which put on oratorios, cantatas and several operas. He directed the Congregational choir for a number of years and was a member of the Ravenna City band for a much longer period. [The story of John Oakley's life was incomplete, because the eulogy failed to mention that John Henry Oakley was a fine Base Ball player and Vice-President of the Ravenna Star Base Ball Club in the glorious summers of 1867 and 1868.] [128]

Col. Charles S. Cotter, a Star Club Director and aspiring pitcher, operated a brass foundry and silver plating business in Ravenna. Prior to the Civil war, Cotter's scientific and military bent led him to form an independent gun battery that performed efficiently at 4th of July celebrations. Cotter's Battery became the nucleus for Battery A, 1st Ohio Light Artillery which served gallantly in the western theater.

Cotter was a fun loving man who had his soldiers to square dance, himself making the calls. Frequently and late at night, the Colonel would collect his best singers from their tents, and the assembly would visit and serenade the wealthy residents near Louisville, Kentucky. In return, the "boys" earned a late night snack and the opportunity to socialize with the local belles. Although in later years the Colonel became a temperance man, in the early 1860's he was known to have a nip from a bottle of "Brave Critters." Yet, Cotter was a skilled and fearless artilleryman with an outstanding servive record, in spite of his confrontations with the West Point regulars. Among Cotter's exploits was his conspicuous conduct at Corinth, being captured and paroled at Perryville, and commanding all of the Union reserve artillery at Chattanooga.

In April 1884, Cotter was deeply involved in an incident which could be filed under "My, how things have changed in Ohio!" The Colonel was enjoying a cushy patronage job as superintendent of state house grounds and laborers under Democratic Gov. George Hoadley. When arson and murderous riot erupted in Cincinnati, the rioters (today's "protesters") stormed the city jail and torched the courthouse. The National Guard was called out, and Gov. Hoadley sent his "Chief of Artillery," Col. C. S. Cotter, to quash the uprising.

In the aftermath of the riot, the newspapers lamented the loss of the splendid Law Library, ancient transcripts, and the stupidity and lawlessness of the rioters and arsonists. Almost as an afterthought, the human tragedy was reported as *39 people killed and nearly 300 wounded.* Cotter's hometown newspaper had this to say about the Colonel's actions.

> Col. C. S. Cotter, Chief of Artillery on the governor's staff and Superintendent of the State house took an active part in putting down the Cincinnati riot, and won high praise for his able and efficient services. He is every inch a soldier.

As for Gov. Hoadley, his days as Ohio's chief executive were numbered, not because of the casualties but because he did not send the troops in *sooner.*

When the Colonel died from a stroke in January 1886, the *Ravenna Republican* presented its view of a political opponent in a frank, honest, and yet respectful report.

Col. Charles S. Cotter with his cap askew strikes a jaunty pose atop Lookout Mountain in March, 1864. Courtesy of the U. S. Military History Institute. Vol. 65, p. 3217B.

...Col. Cotter was recognized everywhere as a "good fellow," one that would divide his last dollar with a friend, and whether his lack of prudence was admired or not, everyone respected his free-handed generosity...Col. Cotter was widely known, and he will be greatly missed.

Somehow a vision persists of Col. Cotter waving his kepi hat and cheering at the top of his lungs as the Union troops advance or as a member of the Star Club rounds third base and legs it toward home to score a tally. [129]

Thomas B. Alcorn taught school in Ravenna and Canton before he attended Michigan University and graduated from its law department. Alcorn then moved to Pittsburgh, Pa., where he became a prominent member of the bar and a widely known Democrat. Tom Alcorn did not forget his friends and relatives of his hometown, as the newspapers often reported his arrival in town on a visit.

After Alcorn died in the Pittsburgh hospital in July of 1915, his obituary stated that he was 63 years old, but cemetery records show that he was 66. His death resulted from complications due to a fractured hip received in a fall on June 27th. Funeral services were held at the family home on Main Street in Ravenna. Tom was survived by his wife, two sons, and a daughter.

[He] had been a resident of Pittsburgh for 35 years. He was prominent in political circles, having held both county and Federal positions. During 1905 and 1906 he held the dual office of county and city chairman, was once a solicitor for the county commissioners at Pittsburgh and was on several occasions a candidate for Judge.

During the first [Grover] Cleveland administration he was assistant to United States Attorney Allen, and was several times a national delegate, helping to nominate Alton B. Parker for president...

Tom Alcorn should have been recognized as a fine infielder for the Ravenna Star Base Ball Club and the winning pitcher in the first contest for the Rosewood Bat and the Silver Ball in 1867. [130]

When it came to their allotted number of life's innings, two members of the Star Club were short-changed. Even when combined, their years did not amount to the proverbial three score and ten. **George E. King**, who had survived the fierce onslaught of Morgan's Raiders in the Civil War, could not survive the attack of disease. George died on June 14, 1881, fourteen years after delivering "swift and well-directed" pitches as well as performing at catcher. His obituary reads as follows:

> George E. King, a young attorney of Ravenna, died at his residence in [the] south-west part of town, Tuesday evening, after a long illness, aged 36 years. He was a young man of fine education and excellent character. He was a native of Ravenna, but for several years had been engaged in the practice of his profession in the city of New York, but on account of failing health, in April last he returned to the home of his childhood to spend his few remaining days. He leaves a wife and two young daughters – one aged five and one two years. – with hosts of friends to mourn his death. The funeral will take place from the family residence, this (Thursday) afternoon at 3 o'clock. [131]

Edward W. Wadsworth, who was an outstanding Base Ball player for the Star Juniors and then as center fielder for the Star Club, certainly was a young man of promise. For E. W. Wadsworth there would be no long list of fraternal memberships, numerous grandchildren to bounce on his knees, or summer days of watching a younger generation play ball on the Fair Grounds. In his short life there was not much time to score runs, make hits, or the opportunity to make errors.

> Death of E. W. Wadsworth. – Last week we briefly announced the illness of Mr. E. W. Wadsworth, and now it becomes our sad duty to chronicle his death. He died at the Anderson House in Eaton Rapids, Michigan at about four o'clock, Friday morning, April 23d, 1875, of consumption of the lungs and bowels. Deceased was the eldest son of the late William Wadsworth. He was born in this town April 7th, 1849, and had just passed the 26th year of his age. He had grown to the years of manhood in our midst, and was a young man of exemplary character and excellent business habits,

and universally loved and esteemed by all who knew him. For something over a year he had been engaged in the hardware business with his uncle at Jacksonville, Ill., where he was well liked. On the 24th of November last he was united in marriage with Miss Dora Martin, of Baltimore, Md., who survives to deeply mourn her sad loss. His remains were brought here on Saturday and his funeral took place at two o'clock Sunday afternoon at the residence of his mother on Prospect street, and was largely attended by sympathising friends. [132]

On a happier note was the longevity of **Isaac J. Vance**, a well-liked old man who was affectionately known to almost everyone in the town. In early February 1908 the 74-year old carpenter was working on a storm door for a lady resident of Ravenna. Perhaps his thoughts turned to the desired and anticipated warmer spring weather and the coming baseball season. Once again, there were a number of fine local teams in the area. Maybe they would be as exciting as the days when Isaac was a slick fielding first and second baseman for the Ravenna Stars. However, Isaac's body crumbled to the ground, his earthly days of baseball and usefulness were over. His passing made front page news in the *Portage County Democrat* – "STROKE PROVES TO BE FATAL., Isaac J. Vance Passes Away After Long Life of Usefulness Spent in Ravenna."

Isaac J. Vance, who was stricken with apoplexy last Tuesday, died on Friday as a result of this stroke. As noted in past week's paper, he was at work on a storm door for Mrs. S. Parmalee at the residence of J. H. Evans on South Chestnut St., when he was stricken, being found there by Mrs. Parmalee.

He was taken to the White hospital, where his condition showed some improvement but he became until death relieved him Friday. Funeral services were held from the home on Cleveland Ave., Monday afternoon, the Masonic lodge having charge of the services. This had been Mr. Vance's request.

Mr. Vance had been a resident of Ravenna for 58 years and was therefore known to almost everyone in town. He was born in Allegheny county, Pa., 74 years ago and moved here when he was a boy of sixteen. He learned the carpenter's trade, later doing considerable contracting work in that line. He was married in 1860 to Miss Matilda J. Ney, Ravenna, who still survives him. Two children were born to them. They are Mrs. Lena Madole and Mrs. Thos. Aitken, California, Pa. For several years during his early life Mr. Vance was in the grocery business with T. L. Parsons of this city. He also served as village marshal for several years at one time. [sic] He had been active in some walk of life and up to the time he was stricken, had been a hard worker. [133]

Not many local Base Ball teams' alumni could boast of having two doctors, unless they were the Asylum Club or a medical college. George Somerville had been a hotshot on the 1867 "Juvenile," team, and in '68 he manned the hot corner (3b) for the Ravenna Stars. When the fifty-five year old bachelor passed away on September 16, 1905, he left a brother, a spinster sister, and a mother who apparently required much attention. George was a good son.

Dr. George Howard Somerville was found dead in bed at his office in Newburg, 254 Broadway on Saturday. Heart failure caused his sudden decease. The remains were brought to Ravenna and buried in maple Grove Tuesday afternoon after brief private service at the home and Masonic service at Maple Grove by his fellow members of Newburg Lodge, F. & A. M., who arrived by special C. & P. train at 2:15 p.m.
Dr. Somerville was born in Ravenna, July 4, 1850, son of George Somerville, now deceased, and of Emily Howard Somerville, who bowed with the weight of many years, survives a devoted son. He is also survived by a brother Charles E. and a sister Miss Lina M. Somerville. The deceased physician graduated from Ravenna schools in 1870 and later from Dickinson College, at Carlisle, Pa. He then read medicine with the late Dr. Joseph Waggoner and graduated from the Western Reserve Medical School at Cleveland. He practiced in Newburg ever since, for 26 years. He was assistant surgeon to Dr. M. L. Brooks at the Cleveand Rolling Mills, the men in which fairly idolized him. Dr. Somerville was never married, giving his entire devotion to his mother and the home family. [134]

Dr. Edgar C. Swain's story evoked memories of freshman literature class and being required to read Edwin Arlington Robinson's poem, "Richard Cory."[135] Christmas Eve, 1903 was not a happy occasion for the doctor's family as the *Ravenna Republican*'s prominent news item attested: "ENDS LIFE BY INHALING GAS." The case had all of the ingredients for a modern day forensics investigation.

...With business declining day by day, and his health failing, Dr. E. C. Swain, one of the well known dentists of Cleveland, committed suicide in his office in the Benedict Bloc, No. 29 Euclid avenue, at an early hour Tuesday morning. He undressed himself, lay down upon a sofa in the office some time during Monday night and threw an overcoat and other covering over him. Then he placed in his mouth the end of a rubber tube which he had previously attached to a gas jet on the side wall. The gas, being turned on, Dr. Swain was soon asphyxiated.

The Benedict Block is a sort of headquarters for dental offices. Dr. L. D. Lindsay, who has an office adjoining, uncovered the smell of gas when he opened his office door Tuesday morning. It evidently came from the office of Dr. Swain. He imagined that Dr. Swain had left the gas turned on by accident when he closed the office on the night before, and therefore he investigated. He peered through the keyhole and saw that Dr. Swain had left his cuffs on the canter table. Then he raised the transom window, and while standing on a chair, saw what appeared to be the lifeless body of the dentist lying upon the sofa. Dr. Lindsay called the custodian of the building and egress to the apartment was obtained. Dr. Swain was dead, although it was evident that death had come only a short time before. His body was still warm.

That it was a case of premeditated suicide was evident from the fact that the tube which was used had been wound with wire close to the jet, so that there would not be a possible chance for it to collapse. Bellstein's ambulance was called and the police were notified at once. No note was left behind. There was absolutely no motive apparent except that Swain had been in bad health and was discouraged on account of business affairs. In a drawer to his table, which stood near the couch, was a revolver. It was loaded, but had not been used.

 Dr. Swain was fifty-four years of age. He leaves a widow and two [grown] children, a son and a daughter... Dr. Swain's home life had always been pleasant, so far as is known, but it is claimed that during the past few days Dr. Swain had acted strangely. He reported to the police Monday that someone had stolen a valuable overcoat from his office. No one seems to have met him after that until the custodian of the Benedict block met him in the hallway Monday evening. The custodian, whose name is Sanderson, claims that Dr. Swain was pacing up and down in the hallway uneasily.

 Dr. Swain had not been home since Sunday. This was the statement which Walter S. Swain [son] made to the police at the investigation. Efforts to locate him [the doctor] had been of no avail. "I cannot but think that my father's mind must have been temporarily unbalanced," he said. "He had been worrying considerable of late. I know of no motive for the suicide other than that he had been suffering from rheumatism considerably."

 Dr. Swain was a warm friend of Dr. D. R. Jennings, who committed suicide several years ago in his office in the Arcade. They were together in an office at Ravenna... [136]

 Edgar Swain was remembered primarily for the method of his demise; however, there certainly had been brighter days for "E. Swain." There had been a time when he was an 18-year old athlete cruising the outfield for the Ravenna Star Club in '67. Then, there was that sublime moment in the summer of 1868 when Swain toed the pitcher's line and hurled his team to the county championship victory over the Hiram Boanerges Club. On that day, Swain also raced around the bases and scored five of his team's 49 tallies.

 Two of the Ravenna Star alumni received only short obituary notices in the hometown newspaper. Still, that was better than the short shrift that other teammates received.

 In late July 1867, **William D. Gardner** broke into the Ravenna Star lineup as the center fielder. His aggressiveness and sure hands soon gained for him the reputation for making great "fly catches." W. D. Gardner finished the 1867 and 1868 seasons as the regular shortstop for the Star Club. Gardner moved out of town to seek his fame and fortune; and in 1925, fifty-seven years after his ball playing days were over, he returned home for the last time. The Ravenna *Republican-Democrat* carried the news on the front page: "BRING BODY OF FORMER RESIDENT FOR BURIAL."

> William Gardner, former resident of Ravenna, passed away at his home in Chicago, Sunday night. The body will arrive in Ravenna on the 906 B. and O. train, Wednesday morning, and services will immediately follow at Maple Grove [cemetery] chapel. Interment will be in the family lot.
> Mr. Gardner left Ravenna over 50 years ago and was superintendent of the steel mills at Joliet, Ill., for many years, following which he removed to Chicago. Mrs. Gardner will accompany her husband's body to this city. [137]

Morton H. Phillips of Washington, D. C. died at the home of his daughter in Toronto, Canada in October of 1917. He was 70 years old. Morton's wife died many years before, and three daughters and his brother George survived him.

The 1880 Census for Ohio listed Phillips as a hotel clerk in Warren, Ohio. Another source has him residing in Philadelphia in 1885. M. H. Phillips' obituary contained no information regarding his occupation or interests; however, it was briefly noted that "The deceased was a civil war veteran and had many friends here." This, in itself, still said much for the man.

It is known that Morton Phillips enjoyed and participated in at least one fraternal organization. He was the secretary and a shortstop for the Ravenna Star Base Ball Club in 1867. [138]

The life of **George M. Phillips** illustrates that timing often is everything. When he was not playing third base, roving the outfield, or keeping score for the Star Club, George worked as a teller at the 2nd National Bank in Ravenna. In April 1868, George took a position as *cashier* at the First National Bank in Northfield, Minnesota.

On September 9, 1876 eight scruffy and dust-covered horsemen with larceny on their minds rode into Northfield. It was the dreaded gang of Jesse and Frank James, and their target was the 2nd National Bank. The bank robbers pointed their six-shooters at the *cashier* and demanded that he open the combination to the vault. When the *cashier* refused to cooperate, one desperado slashed the *cashier's* throat, and another outlaw fired a bullet into the *cashier's* temple. The bank teller, who did not know the combination to the vault, dashed out the back door of the bank under a hail of bullets. The teller received a shoulder wound.

The suspicious strangers and the ensuing gunfire had the effect like poking a hornet's nest with a stick. From their positions in second story windows, doorways, and other hiding places, the aroused citizens of Northfield fought back. An angry posse was quickly formed, and a long, hot pursuit of the fleeing bandits began. Eventually, only Jesse and Frank James escaped the wrath of the determined posse.

Fortunately for George Phillips, the regular *cashier* of the 2nd National Bank, he was out of town on September 9th attending the Centennial Exposition in Philadelphia, Pa. The Ravenna *Republican-Democrat* announced the good news to George's old friends on September 27th.

> Mr. G. M. Phillips, son of T. G. Phillips of Ravenna, cashier of the Northfield (Minn.) Bank, was visiting the Centennial at the time of the recent attempted robbery of his Bank. He returned home at once, and has sent us a very full account of the affair, the substance of which, however, we had already published. During the past week four more of the robbers were captured at Madelia, Minn., after a desperate struggle, one of them being killed and the other three wounded. There are only two more to be captured.

George, who remained a bachelor, retired from the banking business in 1920. He then lived with his sister in Norwalk, Ohio. "Besides being 32nd degree Mason, Mr. Phillips was a member of the national Societies of the Sons of the Colonial Wars and the American Revolution. He served many years as a trustee of Carleton College of Northfield and to his influence and material aid many successful men and women owe their education."

George Phillips died in August of 1932 at the age of 87. He was laid to rest beside his brother Morton. [139]

When **Prof. Allen Campbell Barrows** strode onto the Base Ball field, his mere presence commanded respect. His manifold reputation was that of a gifted athlete, Civil War fighting man, brilliant intellectual, and sterling character. "He was graduated from Western Reserve University with the degree of A. B. in 1861 and five years later [after serving gallantly with the 18th U. S. Infantry in the War of the Rebellion] was given the degree of A. M. by the same institution. He taught Latin and Greek in Phillips' Exeter Academy in 1865; taught physics in Western Reserve from 1866 to 1870 and Latin and English literature in the same university in 1871." His exploits as an athlete in 1866 have been cited in a previous chapter.

One of the Professor's students saw his mentor in the following light.

> Prof. Barrows was a man of wide attainments and great independence and vigor of character. The writer of this was under his instruction daily for more than three years, and gratefully remembers him as an elder brother. Beneath an exterior that at first seemed to repel, beat one of the bravest and most genial of hearts. For indolence, and especially for shirking of duty, he had only withering scorn, which upon occasion he could show in a most uncomfortable way. But given a disposition to work, no student looked to him in vain for justice, encouragement and real helpfulness. If the writer ever absorbed any sense of sarcasm for human inertia, otherwise called laziness, his vocabulary for expressing it was greatly enriched from this source.
>
> Yet he was naturally, and by habit, the gentlest and tenderest of men. He was no recluse either. He was interested in all politics and in whatever touched humanity for its good. His garden was the envy of his townsmen. His grape-vines were the poaching ground of the students, and he was the most noted baseball pitcher of the old Reserve nine.
>
> To go off with Prof. Barrows on a surveying lesson in the spring term, triangulating Mr. Baldwin's big pasture, or over to Boston Ledges, was a privilege and not a task. He simply would not let a student flunk outright in class, but would toll him along very much as a New England farmer does a lot of unwilling sheep through a gap in the fence.

As far as the *Portage County Democrat* was concerned, if Professor Barrows endorsed a product, then that product had to be good. When Barrows was a physics professor in 1869, he tested a

"Gas Machine" and reported his results.

> There is printed in another column a letter from Prof. Barrows of Hudson College, commending the Gas Machine" invented and patented by Mr. H. Wain of Ravenna. This letter is valuable. Prof. Barrows is a practical as well as scientific man. During a period of four weeks he subjected the machine to a variety of tests and trials, and examined it minutely. What he says of it is the result of the most practical and scientific tests. Such testimony places the importance and value of the machine beyond question – and puts its capacity for safety beyond a reasonable doubt.

A. C. Barrows shifted his full attention to the ministry, and he served the Kent Congregational Church for thirteen years. In April 1871, two local "What-Not" items probably drew Barrows' attention.

> The base ballers are in the field again, and another campaign is opening up lively. One of the "champions" had a finger smashed last week, by a red hot ball...
> Prof. Barrows will give the concluding lecture of the Congregational Church course Wednesday evening of this week. A lecture from Prof. Barrows cannot fail to be interesting, and the announcement of his name we have no doubt will draw a full house....

In the early 1880's Barrows would hold his services at the Kent church, and then in the afternoon he would conduct services at the Presbyterian Church in Streetsboro. He was well known and loved in both communities.

Barrows left the ministry and returned to the academic life. "Prof. Barrows then went to Iowa Agricultural College, where he was professor of English literature until 1894. In that year he was elected to the chair of English literature in Ohio State University, which position he held up to the time of his death."

On January 19, 1908 Allen Campbell Barrows died at his home in Columbus; he was 67 years old. "He had been ill of the grip [the grippe, or influenza] about a week, but his condition had not been regarded as dangerous." The Kent local news noted that "His remains were cremated in Cincinnati." [140]

Somewhere in a perfect Heaven, the Ravenna Stars and a host of other "base ballers" are gathered with their teammates on some Elysian field, where a mellow, late afternoon glow bathes the scene which looks remarkably like the old Driving Park. The Ladies of village are nearby in the carriages keeping tally, and the men and boys eagerly crowd the chalk lines. Prof. Barrows, the saintly umpire, strides to home plate, gazes at the angelic faces a moment, and then trumpets, "Play ball!" The heavenly hosts cheer mightily, and God smiles as the Star Club nine trots onto the field to defend their possession of the Rosewood Bat and the Silver Ball.

Someone in this later day Ravenna Star organization must have remembered the first Base Ball Club of the town. The original photograph was discovered in the Copper Kettle Antiques store in Ravenna, Ohio.

CHAPTER NINE

THE LEGACY

Although squinting into the evening sunshine made any fly ball or line drive a potentially dangerous or embarrassing situation, right field was the place to be. The pitcher threw a hard fastball, so the right handed batters swung late; and the action was more than standing around and yelling, "Hey, batter! Hey, Batter." In the waist-high weeds behind the outfield the only spectators were the chirping crickets and some scurrying critters. The "turf" consisted primarily of freshly mowed chickweed and clover, which sent a pleasant aroma into the humid summer air. From his vantage point, the right fielder noticed the lengthening shadows of everyone on the field. Little did he realize then that other young boys and men had cast long shadows, both literally and figuratively, across the community's playing fields in days of yore.

Beyond the left field foul line was the back of the small, brick, country schoolhouse. If a kid *wanted* to learn, this was the place to be. The right fielder was proud to be a part of the old school, even though he had been introduced to the "board of education" no less than three times from three different teachers. Not wanting to improve on that unworthy record, he decided to behave in a more civilized manner. Beyond the right field line, across a field of weeds, and over a clump of trees was a cluster of old homes and the center of the community. Diagonally across the corner from the brick hardware store stood the old wooden tavern, where cold tap beer and words of wisdom copiously flowed.

The best meeting place, however, was the barbershop that was operated by the father-son team of Jim and Ike Williams. For entertaining yarns, an excellent haircut, and customer pampering, Jim's and Ike's barbershop could not be beaten; even the lowliest country bumpkin strode out of the two-chair shop feeling like a prince, or at least a duke. It was a time when a high pompadour and wing-swept sides were in vogue, but this summer the right fielder

MANCHESTER BASEBALL TOWN TEAM--1910
Top row, (left to right): Duffy Carr, Bill Lewis,
Jim Williams, Homer Carmany, Herman Sisler,
Joe Lewis. Bottom row, (left to right): Die Carty,
Otis Carmany, Bill Elsner, Cappy Thomas,
Harry Carmany.

This photograph is pinned on the barbershop wall. This copy is the courtesy of Richard A. Gardner, author of *History of an Ohio Community, Manchester*.

129

The M. O'Neill department store of Akron sponsored this team. Poll-Parrot was the leading brand of shoes. Top row: Frank Norris, Bill Pearson, Ike Williams [a high school sophomore at the time], Coach Andrews, Jack Newton, Mike Feduniak, Joe Peteca. Bottom row: Dom Saconne, Lefty Haun, Ben Semchuck, Bat Boy (Andrews), Beany Lorenzo, Curly Bruggeman, Al Elias.

sported his first crewcut due to being at the barbershop at the wrong time. As the burly, highly esteemed football coach, Swede Olsson, thrust his bulk from Ike's chair, Ike bid the coach a good day and called, "Next." When the right fielder approached the chair, Ike asked, "How do you want it cut?" The Swede butted in and said, "Cut it like mine." Voila! A longtime crewcut fan was born.

In the 1930's Ike Williams had been a slick fielding shortstop/pitcher who had aspirations of reaching the big leagues. However, young Ike got snapped up in the peace time draft of 1940. A five-year military stint ensued, which included a seven-months' battle on Bougainville in the Solomon Islands, which, according to Ike, seemed more like seven years. After his service in the Pacific, Ike returned to Ft. Benning to play service baseball. The fields of Ft. Benning were in far better condition than those of his hometown, thanks to the work of the German P.O.W.'s, who were as happy as larks and free to roam around. Following the war, Ike returned to Manchester, where he started three little league teams and helped to construct new and better diamonds.

Some talented baseball players seem to have the gift to play written in their DNA – the Alou's, Bonds' and DiMaggio's to name but a few. This probably was true in Ike's case. His dad, Jim, had been a smallish pitcher, but he had good pop on his fastball, a sharp breaking curve, and the great asset of pinpoint control. Among Jim's childhood friends in Manchester was one George Harold Sisler.

"Gorgeous George" Sisler was such an outstanding baseball player that he was inducted into the National Baseball Hall of Fame in 1939. Among Sisler's many achievements was a .407 batting average in 1920 and a .420 average two years later. His major league record of 257 base hits in 1920 still stands. Amidst his lifetime average of .340 was a 41-game hitting streak. As a first baseman, George was as quick and agile as a cat. It is no wonder that everyone who was associated with George wanted to claim him for their own. Akron claims him because he was an outstanding athlete and 1911 graduate of old Akron High School. The University of Michigan holds a rightful claim to George. At Ann Arbor he compiled a 50-0 record as a pitcher before graduating in 1915 with a degree in mechanical engineering. Since George played for the St. Louis Browns in the American League and his final resting place is in Richmond, Missouri, the "Show me" state has a viable claim. BUT, Manchester owns the original claim because George Sisler was born

George Sisler

"When George Sisler and the St. Louis Browns came to Old League Park in Cleveland to play the Indians, he would look into the crowd to see if he could find some old friends. In seeing my Dad [Jim Williams] and others, George would walk into the stands and sit with them for awhile."

Ike Williams

in the heart of the community on March 24, 1893, the son of Cassius Sisler, a coal mine manager, and Mary (Whipple) Sisler.[141]

It is a fact that baseball talent also flowed in George's gene pool. In addition, his clean living – he neither smoked nor drank – would have fit the gentlemanly aspect of the majority of the old-time "base ballers." Thus, all of the aforementioned leads us back to the era of the Rosewood Bat and the Silver Ball and the originators of the Manchester legacy. At one time, Manchester was named Nimisila, which means "beautiful water;" and in the summer of 1871 Nimisila fielded a beautiful Base Ball team. On that nine were *three* Sislers.

Base Ball – Nimisillas vs. Amphibians.

A very spirited game of base ball came off of yesterday [July, 25th] at Manchester, between the Nimisillas of that place and the Akron Club, on the grounds of the former. The twelve good little boys left Akron in the forenoon with high hopes and anticipations of a good time, but the rain commenced soon after and falling faithfully slightly damaged their spirits, notwithstanding the enlivening effects of song from McK—y, the nightingale for the occasion. However, on arriving at Manchester and meeting their old friend M. C. Sorrick, of Akron, now visiting there, and a number of the rival club, and after surrounding a square meal at solicitation of "mine host of the inn," (little urging was necessary) they were restored to complete good humor. The game commenced at 2 o'clock and ended at 4:40. Eight innings were played, there was one white-wash on each side. Muffs were too common for so warm a day. The "fielding" was excellent. Several flys were caught and some "was-ups." In one particular the Manchester grounds excel ordinary grounds – in the presence of a hornet's nest in the field, the individual numbers of which evinced a lively interest in the game. An occasional yell from a "fielder" announced the "sending in of hot ones."

During the game the grounds were visited by a bevy of the Manchester beauties, adding interest to the scene. The score, owing to the superiority of the Nimisillas' batting, or else to the inferiority of the batting of the Amphibians, or else to the too diligent handkerchief service by the "umpire" and "scorer," turned out at the conclusion, 63 to 21 in favor of

Nimisilla.

After the game the Club partook of a splendid supper "set up" by the victorious club, and the best of spirits prevailed. After supper our club took their way homeward, quietly and soberly, and perfectly satisfied with their day's enjoyment.

BARRATOR. [142]

After the battle with the country boys and the hornets' nest, it the Akron boys hosted the return match. Without nature's hindrance and with a change of officiating, perhaps they could erase that 42-run deficit in the previous game.

Base Ball.

The Akron Base Ball Club was captured again on Saturday afternoon last, on which occasion they played a match game with their old opponents of Nimisilla. Appended is the

SCORE.

AKRON	O.	R.	MANCHESTER	O.	R.
Courtney, c	4	2	Chas. Sisler, c	3	5
Seward, r.f	2	3	Will Sisler, 2b	3	4
Spafford, s.s	3	1	Emmons, 1b	3	4
Glick, 1b	2	3	Keller, l.f	3	5
Iredell, c.f	2	2	Marsh, r.f	2	5
Smith, p	3	2	Benner, 3b	4	4
Noble, l.f	4	1	Spangler, c.f	4	4
Brown, 3b	4	2	Marsh Sorrick, p	4	7
Hopfman, 2b	3	3	Cad Sisler, s.s	4	4
Total	27	19	Total	27	42
Fly catches		12	Fly catches		9
Muffed balls		5	Muffed balls		8

INNINGS

	1	2	3	4	5	6	7	8	9	Total
Akrons	1	4	2	1	6	0	4	0	1	19
Manchesters	8	5	18	5	4	1	0	0	1	42

Umpire, Louis D. Seward.
Scorers, Geo. H. Jessup, Cal. Kauffman.
Time of game, 2h, 39m.

The game was played on the Good [Park] grounds, quite a crowd gathering to witness it. Everything passed off pleasantly on the grounds, as well as at the Empire House, where the visitors were served with supper...[143]

As witnessed in the numerous Base Ball accounts herein, the National pastime once had a terrific sense of humor in its legacy. On an early May day in the 1870's, the chipper editor of Ravenna's *Democratic Press* waxed humorously on a number of subjects, to wit:

A LITTLE boy was asked the other day if he knew where the wicked finally went to. He answered: "They practice law a spell here and then go to the legislature." It was a painful thing for that boy to sit down for a few days. [144]

In his repertoire of springtime humor, Mr. Editor also reprinted a Base Ball anecdote written by Kate Thorn for the *New York Weekly.*

Base-Ball Playing.

We are not going to say a word against it. Oh, no. The boys would not like it. It is all the go just now. It is more in repute than horse-racing or any other diversion.

Every young man who aspires "to be anything" has got a set of striped stockings, a tri-colored cap, and a pair of tights, which he calls his uniform. In this uniform he develops his muscle.

To get muscle is the thing nowadays, but it is not gained in the old-fashioned way. In the days of our grandparents nobody dreamed of getting strong by swinging from trapezes, jumping over poles, or playing base-ball. Muscle was mostly obtained, in those days, by following the plow., swinging the scythe, and performing with a good wood-saw on the winter's fuel.

Base-ball playing is one of the most approved methods of getting muscle.

We freely confess that we know nothing about the game. We are in profound ignorance as to "pitches," "catches," and "innings" and et cetera. We have seen the game played hundreds of times, and we know just as much about it as we did when we were a baby.

But the players enjoy it. People go to see them play who know just as much about the game as we do, and they call it "splendid," and of course it is. How the local paper sets forth in glowing colors the triumph of its own town club, and how all the friends and relatives of the various members of that club purchase the paper and send it to friends and relatives at a distance that they may know that the Stool Oaks have beaten the Drooping Willows by so many runs.

Through hot and cold, wet and dry, storm and sunshine, your genuine base-ballist will play his favorite game.

The frost may purple his nose, and the sun may broil him alive in his uniform, but he will not give up. The balls will very likely miss their aim and hit somebody on the skull, and crash in somebody's nasal organ, or stop an eye here and there, but none of the club take warning thereby. Accidents, they say will happen everywhere. A man is just as likely to get his eyes bung [sic] by hoeing corn, or laying bricks, as he is at base-ball playing. Who is going to give up a noble game because he gets a little hit now and then?

All other business has to yield to base-ball playing.

Does mother want Tom to help her about any household job? Tom looks at her in amazement. Does not she know that he has got to play ball? Does father need him about making things snug for winter, why, the world must wait. Tom's club meets that very day to see about playing a game with the Drooping Willow Club.

The uniforms claim a great deal of attention, and the sisters of these base-ballists have to lay aside their crochet and tattings, and attend to demoralized tights and twisted stockings, and champion belts.

And though cheeks be bruised from blows of bats and random balls, and hands be swelled to twice the size designated by nature, the boys do not mind it.

"Our Club beat 'em," and that is glory enough. [145]

Through rose-tinted memories, some folks long for the so-called "good old days," but this was not the intent of the *Days of the Rosewood Bat and the Silver Ball*. True, the text resembles Memorial Day in some respects, but the observance of Thanksgiving Day is more appropriate here because it is a celebration for the blessings, which we have received.

Ike Williams says that cutting hair is like being an artist; you have to know when to stop. The same holds true for spinners of Base Ball stories.

Judging by the equipment and the "H" and "WRA" on the shirts, could these be the grandsons of the renowned Enterprise or Reserve Clubs? Courtesy of Gwen Mayer and the Hudson Library Archives.

FOOTNOTES

1. Walter J. Dickinson, *Pioneer History, 1802-1865* (Ravenna, Ohio : Record Publishing Company, 1953), 69.
2. *Summit Beacon* (Akron, Ohio), July 6, 1853.
3. *Portage Sentinel* (Ravenna, Ohio), July 5, 1854.
4. John Montgomery Ward, *Base-Ball, How To Become A Player with the Origin, History, And Explanation Of The Game* (Philadelphia: The Athletic Publishing Company, 1888), 13.
5. Dickinson, 69. Walter J. Dickinson was born on January 27, 1832; however, he placed his July 4th and "ball" remembrances in a section that was titled: "Chapter VIII, Clothes, Food, Log Cabins, And Customs (1802-1830)." 59-72. He may have been relating a story that had been told to him. The other possibility is that he placed his childhood memory in the wrong time slot.
6. Ed Folsom, *Walt Whitman's Native Interpretations* (Cambridge: Cambridge University Press, 1994), 35; Allison Caveglia Barash, "Base Ball In The Civil War," *The Base Ball Player's Chronicle*, Volume 2, Summer 2000. Printed by the Vintage Base Ball Association, Communications Committee, John Freyer, 9209 S. Central, Oak Lawn, Ill., 60453.
7. Folsom, 42.
8. Folsom, 53.
9. Emanuel Hertz, *The Hidden Lincoln* (Garden City, New York: Blue Ribbon Books, 1940), 379. "The game of fives (hand ball) is what no one despises who has ever played it. It is the finest exercise for the body and the best relaxation for the mind. He who takes to playing at fives is twice young." William Hazlett 1819." Pete Tyson and Leeann Tyson, "Teaching Handball in the Secondary Schools," 1987, cohandball.com.
10. *Portage County Democrat* (Ravenna, Ohio), April 10, 1861.
11. *Democrat*, April 17, 1861.
12. Henry Chadwick, *Beadle's Dime Base-Ball Player* (New York: Irwin P. Beadle & Co., 1861), 6.
13. *Ibid*. 9.
14. David R. Phillips, *That Old Ball Game* (Chicago : Henry Regnery

Company, 1975), 1.
15. Chadwick, *Beadle's*, 11-16.
16. *Ibid.* 9.
17. *Democrat*, August 21, 1861.
18. *Official Roster of the Soldiers Of The State Of Ohio in the War Of The Rebellion, 1861-1866* (Cincinnati : Ohio Valley Company, 1889), Vol. 8, 492.
19. *Official Roster of Soldiers*, Morton H. Phillips in Vol. 6, 121; George E. King, Vol. 9, 431.
20. *History of Portage County, Ohio, Illustrated 1885* (Chicago: Warner, Beers & Co., 1885; (Ravenna: The Portage County Historical Society, Inc., 1972), 841-842.
21. John W. Stepp and I. William Hill, *Mirrors of War, The Washington Star reports the Civil War* (1961), 133.
22. John S. Bowman and Joel Boso, *The Pictorial History of Baseball* (New York : Gallery Books, 1986), 16.
23. Bell Irwin Wiley, *The Life of Billy Yank* (Garden City: Doubleday & Company, Inc., 1971), 170.
24. James I. Robertson, Jr., *Soldiers Blue and Gray* (Columbia, S.C: University of South Carolina Press, 1988), 88.
25. Geoffrey C. Ward and Ken Burns, *Baseball, An Illustrated History* (New York : Alfred A. Knopf, Inc., 1994), 13.
26. Frederick H. Dyer, *A Compendium of the War of the Rebellion* (Cedar Rapids, Iowa: Torch Press,1908), 1715.
27. "The Historical Game of Rolley-Hole," The Marble Museum, marblemuseum.org/games/roleyhole.html. This site gives the history, rules, and game procedures of rolley-hole marbles.
28. *Summit Beacon*, June 21, 1866.
29. *Western Reserve Chronicle* (Warren, Ohio), September 22, 1866.
30. *Chronicle*, August 22, 1866.
31. *Chronicle*, August 29, 1866.
32. *Ibid.*
33. *Chronicle*, September 12, 1866.
34. *Chronicle*, September 19, 1866.
35. *Summit Beacon*, October 18, 1866.
36. *Ibid.*
37. *Summit Beacon*, August 1, 1867.
38. *Ibid.*
39. *Chronicle*, August 29, 1866.
40. *Chronicle*, June 5, 1867.

41. Joseph Wallace, *The Baseball Anthology* (New York: Harry N. Abrams, Inc., 1994), 61. From Albert G. Spaulding's *America's National Game* (1911).
42. *Summit Beacon*, June 13, 1867.
43. *Democrat*, October 9, 1867.
44. *Summit Beacon*, September 12, 1867.
45. *Democrat*, September 25, 1867.
46. *Chronicle*, August 28, 1867.
47. *Democrat*, October 30, 1867.
48. *Democrat*, November 6, 1867.
49. *Summit Beacon*, September 12, 1867.
50. *Summit Beacon*, July 18, 1867.
51. *Summit Beacon*, August 15, 1867.
52. *Chronicle*, July 17, 1867.
53. *Chronicle*, June 5, 1867.
54. *Chronicle*, July 3, 1867.
55. *Democrat*, October 9, 1867.
56. *Summit Beacon*, May 23, 1867.
57. *Ibid*.
58. *Summit Beacon*, June 27, 1867.
59. *Cleveland Morning Leader* (Cleveland, Ohio), June 29, 1867.
60. *Summit Beacon*, August 15, 1867.
61. *Summit Beacon*, August 1, 1867.
62. *Cleveland Morning Leader*, August 15, 1867.
63. *Morning Leader*, August 16, 1867.
64. *Summit Beacon*, August 22, 1867.
65. *Summit Beacon*, August 29, 1867.
66. *Summit Beacon*, October 17, 1867. The definition for "muffin" is found in *Random House Historical Dictionary of American Slang*, Vol. 2, H-O, J.E. Lightner, Editor (New York : Random House, 1997), 611.
67. *Summit Beacon*, October 31, 1867.
68. *Summit Beacon*, November 7 and 14, 1867.
69. *Democrat*. April 24, 1867.
70. *History of Portage County, Ohio*, 858. Biographical information for Robert B. Witter.
71. *Ravenna Republican*, (Ravenna, Ohio), February 16, 1919. 1. Obituary for John H. Oakley.
72. *Ravenna Republican*, October 4, 1917. Obituary for M.H. Phillips.

73. *Ravenna Republican,* July 22. 1915. Obituary for Thomas B. Alcorn.
74. Cyrus T. Plough, *1874-1978 Bicentennial Atlas of Portage County, Ohio* (Ravenna :The Portage County Historical Society, Inc., 1978) A154. *History of Portage County*, 386.
75. *Ravenna Republican,* October 11, 1917. Obituary for D. C. Coolman.
76. *Democrat,* May 8, 1867.
77. *Ibid.*
78. *Democrat.* June 12, 1867.
79. *Democrat,* June 19, 1867.
80. *Democrat,* June 26, 1867.
81. *Ibid.*
82. *Democrat,* July 17, 1867.
83. *Democrat,* July 24 and 31, 1867.
84. *Summit Beacon,* August 22, 1867, and *The Portage Democrat,* August 14, 1867.
85. *Democrat.* August 21, 1867.
86. *Democrat.* August 28, 1867.
87. *Ibid.*
88. *Democrat,* September 4, 1867.
89. *Democrat,* September 25, 1867. The complete report of the Portage County Fair.
90. *Ibid.*
91. *Democrat,* October 9, 1867.
92. *Democrat,* October 16, 1867.
93. *Democrat,* October 23, 1867.
94. *Democrat,* October 30, 1867.
95. *Democrat,* November 20, 1867.
96. *Ibid.*
97. *Summit Beacon,* April 16, 1868.
98. *Summit Beacon,* May 14, 1868.
99. *Western Reserve Chronicle,* May 27, 1868.
100. *Summit Beacon,* July 2, 1868.
101. *Summit Beacon,* September 17, 1868.
102. *Summit Beacon,* September 24, 1868.
103. *Summit Beacon,* August 21, 1868.
104. *Summit Beacon,* August 27, 1868.
105. *Summit Beacon,* August 13 and September 3, 1868.
106. *Summit Beacon,* August 27, 1868.

141

107. *Summit Beacon*, September 3 and 10, 1868.
108. *Summit Beacon*, July 30, 1868. Other games between "Fats and Leans" were played in the area, i.e., "The Newburgh Game," *Cleveland Leader*, July 22, 1869.
109. *Summit Beacon*, August 13 and 20, 1868.
110. *Hall's General Directory and Business Guide of The City of Akron for 1868-1869*. Compiled from Andrew J. Hall, Publisher of Directories, (Akron: Lane, Canfield & Co., Printers, 1868), 29.
111. *Summit Beacon*, August 13, 1868.
112. *Encarta.msn.com*. Negro League Baseball.
113. *Summit Beacon*, August 20, 1868.
114. *Democrat*, June 24, 1868.
115. *Democrat*, July 8, 1868.
116. *Democrat*, August 19, 1868.
117. *Democrat*, August 28, 1868.
118. *Democrat*, September 9, 1868.
119. *Hiram Student* (Hiram, Ohio), August, 1869. Hiram College Archives.
120. *Hiram Student*, October, 1869. Hiram College Archives.
121. *Democrat*, July 28, 1869.
122. *Leader*, May 11, 1869.
123. *Leader*, June 26, 1869. The game between the Forest City and the Re-serves appears in July 2, 1869.
124. *Leader*, June 19, 1869.
125. *Leader*, June 2, 1869.
126. *Leader*, June 3, 1869.
127. *Democratic Press* (Ravenna, Ohio), May 17, 1893; *History of Portage County*, 858; *Republican-Democrat*, May 3, 1876.
128. *Ravenna Republican*, February 16, 1919, 1.
129. *Democratic Press*, January 21, 1886. Also see Richard J. Staats, *A Grassroots History of the American Civil War, Volume III, Captain Cotter's Battery* (Bowie, Md: Heritage Books, Inc., 2002).
130. *Ravenna Republican*, July 22, 1915, 1.
131. *Democratic Press*, June 16, 1881.
132. *Democrat*, April 29, 1875.
133. *Portage County Democrat* (Ravenna, Ohio), February 13, 1908.
134. *Ravenna Republican*, September 21, 1905.
135. Edwin Arlington Robinson (1869-1935). Richard Cory seemed to be the ideal gentleman in every way. The last two stanzas of Robinson's poem show the sophisticated veneer and the hidden dark

side of Richard Cory. "And he was rich, -- yes, richer than a king, -- And admirably schooled in every grace; In fine, we thought he was everything To make us wish we were in his place./ So on we worked, and waited for the light, And went without the meat, and cursed the bread; And Richard Cory, one calm summer night, Went home and put a bullet through his head." Serve.com/Lucius/Robinsonindex.html.

136. *Ravenna Republican*, December 24, 1903.

137. *Ravenna Republican*, June 16, 1925, 1.

138. *Ravenna Republican*, October 4, 1917, 5.

139. *Evening Record* (Ravenna, Ohio), August 19, 1932.

140. *Democrat*, January 30, 1908; *Ravenna Republican*, January 30, 1908; *Democrat*, July 28, 1869 and April 26, 1871. Hudson Library Archives genealogy files.

141. David L. Porter, Editor, *Bibliographical Dictionary of American Sports. Baseball* (Westport, Conn: Greenwood Press, 2000), 1421-22.

142. *Summit Beacon*, July 26, 1871.

143. *Summit Beacon*, August 2, 1871.

144. *Democratic Press*, May 3, 1877.

145. *Ibid.*

BIBLIOGRAPHY

Dickinson, Walter J. *Pioneer History, 1802-1865*. Ravenna, Ohio: Record Publishing Company, 1953.
Barash, Allison Caveglia. *The Base Ball Player's Chronicle, Volume 2, Summer 2000*. Oak Lawn, Ill.: Vintage Base Ball Association.
Bowman, John S. and Joel Boso. *The Pictorial History of Baseball*. New York: Gallery Books, 1986.
Chadwick, Henry. *Beadle's Dime Base-Ball Player*. New York: Irwin P. Beadle & Co., 1861.
Dyer, Frederick H. *A Compendium of the War of the Rebellion*. Cedar Rapids, Iowa: Torch Press, 1908.
Encarta.msn.com. Negro League Baseball.
Folsom, Ed. *Walt Whitman's Native Interpretations*. Cambridge: Cambridge University Press, 1994.
Hall, Andrew J. *Hall's General Directory and General Business Guide of the City of Akron for 1868-1869*. Akron: Lane, Canfield & Co., Printers, 1868.
Hertz, Emanuel. *The Hidden Lincoln*. Garden City, New York: Blue Ribbon Books, 1940.
History of Portage County, Ohio, Illustrated 1885. Chicago" Warner, Beers & Co., 1885. Ravenna: The Portage County Historical Society, Inc., 1972.
Lightner, J. E., Editor. *Random House Historical Dictionary of American Slang, Vol. 2, H-O*. New York: Random House, 1997.
Marblemuseum.org.org/games/roleyhole.html.
Official Roster of the Soldiers Of The State Of Ohio in the War Of The Rebellion, 1861-1866, Volumes 8 and 9. Cincinnati: Ohio Valley Company, 1889.
Phillips, David R. *That Old Ball Game*. Chicago: Henry Regnery Company, 1975.
Plough, Cyrus T. *1874-1978 Bicentennial Atlas of Portage County, Ohio*. Ravenna: The Portage County Historical Society, Inc., 1978.
Porter, David L. *Bibliographical Dictionary of American Sports, Baseball*. Westport, Conn.: Greenwood Press, 2000.
Robertson, James I., Jr. *Soldiers Blue and Gray*. Columbia, S. C.:

University of South Carolina Press, 1988.
Stepp, John W. and I. William Hill. *Mirrors of War, The Washington Star reports the Civil War*, 1961.
Wallace, Joseph. *The Baseball Anthology*. New York: Harry N. Abrams, Inc., 1994.
Ward, Geoffrey C. and Ken Burns. *Baseball, An Illustrated History*. New York: Alfred A Knopf, Inc., 1994.
Ward, John Montgomery. *Base-Ball, How To Become A Player with the Origin, History, And Explanation Of The Game*. Philadelphia: The Athletic Publishing Company, 1888.
Wiley, Bell Irwin. *The Life of Billy Yank*. Garden City: Doubleday & Company, Inc., 1971.

NEWSPAPERS

Democratic Press. Ravenna, Ohio.
Evening Record. Ravenna, Ohio.
Hiram Student. Hiram, Ohio.
Morning Leader. Cleveland, Ohio.
Portage County Democrat. Ravenna, Ohio.
Portage County Sentinel. Ravenna, Ohio.
Ravenna Republican. Ravenna, Ohio.
Republican Democrat. Ravenna, Ohio.
Summit Beacon. Akron, Ohio.
Western Reserve Chronicle. Warren, Ohio.

TEAM INDEX
Base Ball Clubs prior to 1872.

Active (Kent, O.) 33
Akrons (Akron, O.) 36 43
  52-56 59 81 83 85-87 90
  132-134
Alpines (Wadsworth, O.) 88
Asylum (Newburgh, O.) 34 35
Bloomfield, O. 24 33
Boanerges (Hiram, O.) 97-99
  101-103 105 108
Brecksville, O. 60
Bristol, O. 21 22 33 Farmers
  31 37 38
Buckeyes (Akron, O.) 90
Buckeyes (Cleveland, O.) 104
Buckeyes (Streetsboro, O.)
  76-80 95-97
Delphic Society (Hiram, O.)
  33 34
Duryea's Zouaves 16
Enterprise (Hudson,).) 27
  64-66 68-70
Eureka (Cleveland, O.) 103
Excelsiors (Cleveland, O.) 27
Excelsiors (Philadelphia, Pa.)
  93
Fats (Akron, O.) 89 91 92
Finishers (Akron, O.) 87
Forest Citys (Cleveland, O.)
  17-19 43-56 105-108
Grand River (Austinburg, O.)
  38
Gustavus, O. 24 26 27 31
  36 37
Hesperian Society (Hiram, O.)
  33 34
Independents (Gustavus, O.)
  31 37 38
Independents (Hudson, O.)
  93

Iron Club (Newburgh, O.) 34 35
Island (Kent, O.) 72-76
Jockey (Hiram, O.) 104
Kinsman, O. 24 26 27 31
Knickerbickers (N.Y.) 15
Leans (Akron, O.) 89 91 92
Ledge (Nelson, O.) 72
Lightfoots (Chardon, O.) 103
Mahoning (Warren, O.) 22-24
  26 36 37 66-68
Massachusetts, 13th Regt. 17
Mechanics (Akron, O.) 34
Middleburg (Akron, O.) 86
Molders (Akron, O.) 87
Museum (Akron, O.) 34
Mutuals (East Liberty, Pa.)
  86 87 97-101
Nationals (Wash., DC) 16
New York, 104th Regt. 17
New York, 165th Vol. Inf. 16
Nimisillas (Manchester, O.)
  132-134
Occidentals (Cleveland, O.)
  41 42
Ohio, 6th Artillery Bat. 88
Ohio, 104th O.V.I. 88
Old Persimmons (Tallmadge,
  O.) 88
Olympics (Hudson, O.) 27 41
  42 56 104
Peerless (Sharon, Pa.) 22-24
  26
Penfield Club (Oberlin, O.)
  19 44
Peninsula, O. 60
Political (Kent, O.) 32 33
Potters (Akron, O.) 88
Potters (Mogadore, O.) 88
Railway Union (Cleve.) 44 45

Red Stockings (Cincinnati, O.) 106-108
Reserves (Hudson, O.) 17-19 43-52 55-57 59 84 85 105
Resolutes (Akron, O.) 88 90
Second Nationals (Akron, O.) 93
Starks (Canton, O.) 36
Stars (Ravenna, O.) 7 15 61-80 95-102 109-122
Stars Juniors (Ravenna, O.) 33 103 104
Summit (Cuyahoga Falls, O.) 27
Tyrolean (Harrisburgh, Pa.) 30
Unions (Akron, O.) 34
Uniques (Philadelphia, Pa.) 93
Vermont, 8th Regt. 17
Vermont, 114th Regt. 17
Washingtons (Wash., DC) 16

PLAYERS INDEX
(Players, Scorers, and Umpires prior to 1872)

ABBEY, H. E. 89 91
ALCORN, T. B. 61 62 64 65
  68 72 73 75-79 115 116
ALLISON, 105
ANDREWS, 67
ANGEL, 55
ASHMUN, Dr. 83
ASHTON, 23, John 24
  Wm 23
AUL, W. F. 87 W P 100
BABCOCK, 31 54 87
  W C 83
BALDWIN, 91 Capt. A. P. 88
  J N 89
BAILY, 38
BAIRD, W. 87
BARB, 38
BARNES, Capt. 37 38
BARROWS, A. C. 17 19 20
  45-49 51 69 122-125
BENNER, 133
BENTLY, 78 79 97
BICKEL, 105
BIRCHARD, 23
BIRRELL, Capt. 26
BISHOP, A. 65 G. 68 69
  N. 69
BISHOP, Capt. 24
BLACKMAN, 69
BOCO, 73 75 76
BOLTON, 19
BONNELL, 65 69
BOSWORTH, B. 89 91
BRAINARD, 38
BROOKS, 46-49 51 1 55
BROWN, 46-49 51 54 133
BUCHTEL, 55 John 31 J D
  89 91
BURTON, C. G. 23 24

BUTLER, 68 73 75 76 96 97
  100-102
CAMPBELL, O. J. 64 65 97 98
CARR, H. I. 89 91 92
CATLIN, 75 76
CASE, 38 (Streetsboro) 78 79 97
CASTLE, S. W. 100
CLARK, 19 45-49 51 54
CLASSON, 73
COLLINS, 68 73-75 76 78
COOLMAN, E. B. 61 62 64 65
  68 73 75 76 78 79 100-102
COTTER, C. S. 61 62 67
  112-115
COURTNEY, 133
CRAWFORD, S. S. 79 97
COWDEN, 38
CURTIS, 85
CURTISS, 19
CUTLER, M. T. 89 91
DAY, Wm. R. 68
DUDLEY, 101
EDDY, 19
EMMONS, 133
EWALT, 73 75 C 72
FARR, 101
FENTON, 38
FISHER, J. M. 19
FITCH, 19 67
FOOT, 97
FUNK, 87
GARDNER, Wm. D. 67 97
  100-102 120
GAY, 23
GEORGE, H. 73 75 S 72-76
GERTY, A. P. 52
GLICK, 133
GOODHUE, N. W. 89 91
GORHAM, 19 46-49 51 55

GRAY 67
GRIFFITHS, Mr. 35
HALL, J. J. 89 91
HANDFORD, 19
HANFORD, 85 F 55 Fred 55
  F A 100-102
HANSCOM, 55
HARDY, 23
HARRINGTON, 23
HARRINGTON, (Hudson)
  46-49 51
HARRIS, 68 75 78 79
HART, 38
HARVEY, 18 46-49 51
HASKELL, 46-49 51
HATCH, 31
HATFIELD, E. P. 23 24
HATHAWAY, 38
HAVEN, 87 B 100
HAWKINS, Mr. 24
HEPBURN, 73
HERRINGTON, 85
HEZLEP, 67
HIBBS, 16
HITCHCOCK, H. P. 89 91
HOFFMAN, 73
HOLCOMB, J. W. 66 97
  W 69
HOOPER, E. A. 52 81-83 88
  89 91 92
HOOR, R. F. 89 91
HOPFMAN, 133
HOUSE, Capt. 37 38
HOWARD, 67 68
HOWE, C. R. 83
HUDSON, 54
HUGHES, 23
HUMPHREY, 97
HUNKER, 19 45-49 51, A. H.
  72 74

HUNT, 67
HURLBURT, 19 46-49 51 55
IDDINGS, S. C. 23
INGERSOLL, W. K. 89 91
IREDELL, 133
JACOBS, W. C. 89
JAQUA, Star 65 69
JENKINS, 78 79 97
JESSUP, Geo. H. 133
JOHNSON, 16 (Akron) 91
  (Cleve.) 105
JOHNSTON, C. 89
KAUFFMAN, Cal. 133
KELLER, 133
KELSOO, 32 34
KENNAN, 19 45-49 51
KENT, 72 73
KETCHUM, 18 19
KING, 68 76 78 79 Geo. E 16
  116 Ed. 68
KINSMAN, 67 68
KLINE, 32 34
KOCH, J. 89 91
LANTERMAN, 23
LATIMER, 85
LAUTERMAN, 67 68
LEFFINGWELL, (Hudson) 19
  (Ravenna) 75 78 79
LEHMAN, 85
LOOMIS, 38
LYLE, 87 H T 100
MACK, 87 A J 65
MAHANNAH, 23
MALONE, 85 87
MARR, 16
MARTIN, 87 Jno. 100
MARSH, 133
MASON, 67
MASTERS, W. U. 102
MAYHEW, 38

McBAIN, 78 79
McEBRIGHT, T. 89
McEWEN, 19 46-49 51 54
McHERREN, 16
McINTIRE, 16
McKELVEY, Jno. 87 100 N 87 S M 87 100 W F 100
McKINNEY, H. 89 91
McNULTY, R. 87
MELLEN, 78 96
METLIN, 72-74
MILES, 19
MOORE, 91 M. 65 Milton 89
MOREY, 38
MOUNTS, 23
MUSSON, 73 75 76 78
MYERS, 87 Wm 101
NEY, 73 75 76 78 96 97 100-102
NOBLE, 133
OAKLEY, John H. 16 61 62 64 66 67 69 73 75 78 79 97 100-102 110-112
OVIATT, F. 65 69 J 65 69 M 65 68
PALMER, A. W. 83
PARKER, 38
PATTON, W. W. 32
PAYNE, W. H. 89 91 92
PECK, 78 96
PERKINS, G. T. 83
PHILLIPS, Geo. M. 15 64 67 76 79 121 122
PHILLIPS, (Kent) 72 73 75 76
PHILLIPS, Morton H. 15 61 62 64 65 67 70 74 97 102 121
PIERONG, 85 87
POTTER, 16
POW, 101

POWELL, M. D. 31
PRATT, 105
PROCTOR, 101 102
RANNEY, 67
RAWSON, 55 86 87 E B 83
RAYMOND, W. B. 89 91
REED, 65 68
RICHARDS, 75 76
RIDDLE, 23
ROBERTS, Capt. 26
ROBINSON, G. F. 69 W G 89 91
RODIFER, 101 102
ROLAND, 75 76
SAGER, 38
SCALES, W. 42
SCATES, 46-49 51 55
SCOTT, 87
SEWARD, 133 Lewis D 133
SEYMOUR, 65 69 J 27 J H 79
SHARETS, 16
SHEETS, 85 87
SHERMAN, 23
SISLER, Cad. 133 Chas. 133 Will 133
SMITH, (Akron) 32 34 133
SMITH, (Hudson) 47-49 51 54 85
SMITH, (Warren) 23
SOMERVILLE, Dr. Geo. Howard 96 97 100-102 118
SORRICK, Marsh 133
SPAFFORD, 133
SPANGLER, 133
SQUIRE, 101 102
STOCKLEY, 19 46-49 51 55
STOFFER, 75
STOOK, 78
SULLIVAN, 76 M M 74
SUMNER, J. A. 89 91
SWAIN, Edgar C. 64 65 68 73 96 97 100-102 119 120

TALLMAN, 19
TAYLOR, 23, 67 68
TOMER, 87 100
TRUESDALE, 46-49 51 55
VANCE, I. J. 64 65 67 117
　118
VANTROT, 23
WADSWORTH, Edw. W. 64
　65 68 116 117
WALDEN, 16
WARD, 105
WEBBER, J. B. 64 65 68 73
　96 97 100-102
WEIMER, Geo. 89 91
WHEELOCK, C. F. 76
WHISTON, 38
WHITAKER, 78 79
WHITE, 38
WICKS, 97
WILCOX, 78 79 97 J 101 102
　L 101 102
WITTER, Robert B. 61 62
　64-68 109-111
WOODWORTH, Mr. 26
WORMCASTLE, 87
VILAS, 19
WILLIAMS, 46-49 51
WILSON, 19

GENERAL INDEX

AITKEN, Mrs. Thomas 118
AKRON BLACK SOX, 10 25 40 94
ANDREWS, Coach 129
  Bat Boy 129
BASE BALL CONVENTION, first 8
BELL, Carol Willsey ix
BRAINARD, E. P. 104
BROOKS, Dr. M. L. 118
BROWN, Chas. 89 92
BRUGGEMAN, Curly 129
CLAUR, H. S. 32
CARMANY, Harry 128 Homer 128 Jim vii Otis 128
CARR, Duffy 128
CARTWRIGHT, Alex. Joy 15
CARTY, Die 128
CHADWICK, Henry 8 14 15
CINCINNATI RIOT, 113
CIVIL WAR BASEBALL, 16 17
COOLMAN, D. C. 62 110
DALTON, Dr. 32
DAVIS, Roger vii
DICKINSON, Walter J. 2 3
DUDLEY, Jimmy v
EIERMAN, 40
ELIAS, Al 129
ELIOT, Michael ix
ELSNER, Bill 128
FEDUNIAK, Mike 129
FOREST CITYS, Chagrin Falls 50
FRAZER, Col. Wm. R. 104
GARDNER, Richard A. ix 128
GARFIELD, Jas. A. 103
GAULT, Shane 40
GAYNOR, Cindy ix

GILBERT, Mrs. 22
GILLETTE, Col. R. A. 66
GRANT, Jesse R. 104
HALL, Lyman W. 95
HANDBALL, 5
HARRISSONBURGH, Pa. 30
HAUN, Lefty 129
HAWKINS, Eber 89
HEPPNER, Mark ix
HERALD, Cathy 40
HERLEVI, Marie Karas ix
HERRICK & CANNON, 82 83
HOADLEY, Gov. 113
HOLE MARBLE, 19 20
HOLMES, Dr. Oliver Wendel 2
HORR, Isadore E. 112
HUDSON TEAM, 136
INJURIES, 31 32 83 84
JAMES, Frank and Jesse 121 122
JENNINGS, Dr. D. R. 120
JOHNSON, Lisa ix
JOHNSON'S ISLAND, 15
KING, Jeff vii
KURLICH, Richard vii
LAMBERT, Tom vii
LENT, Tom vii
LEWIS, Bill 128 Joe 128
LINCOLN, Abraham 4 5
LINDSEY, Dr. L. D. 119
LING, Jim vii
LINSEY, Mr. 24
LOOKOUT MT., 114
LORENZO, Beany 129
LUBRANO, Carmen 10
MADOLE, Lena 118
MAIMONE, Chas. ix
MANCHESTER TEAM, (1910) 128
MANCHESTER TEAM, (1954) vii

MARTIN, Geo. W. 89 Dora 117
MAYER, Gwen ix
McNEIL, 90
MEEK, Rev. S. W. 110
MOFFAT, Dr. 32
MORGAN, Gen. John Hunt 16
MUFFIN, 57
MURPHY, T. W. 32
NEWTON, Jack 129
NEY, Matilda J. 118
NORRIS, 129
OHIO MILITARY, 7th OVI 16 111 14th Natl. Guard 16 39th OVI 15 128th OVI 15 171st OVI 16 1st OVLA 16 Bat. A 112 Bat. I 111
OLLSON, Swede 130
PARKER, Alton B. 115
PARMALEE, Mrs. S. 117
PARSONS, T. L. 118
PEARSON, Bill 129
PELTON, L. 26 Mr. & Mrs. 27
PERRY, Gaylord 5
PETECA, Joe 129
PHILLIPS, T. G. 122
POLL PARROT TEAM, (1935) 129
PRIZES, bats and balls 8 24 35 44 53 Rosewood Bat and Silver Ball viii 70 74 76 95 96 cash 39 86
PROFESSIONAL BASEBALL, 104-108
PULFORD, R. D. 32
QUEEN, Dave vii
RAVENNA STAR TEAM, 136
RED STOCKINGS, Cincinnati

RED STOCKINGS (continued) 106-108
RULES, 8-14 29-31 Beadles viii 7-9 11-14 amended 29 30 humorous 30 31
SACONNE, Dom 129
SCHNEIDER, Col. 36
SEARL, Ed 58 Robert 58 Tommy 58
SEMCHUCK, Ben 129
SHIELDS, A. G. 89
SILKNITTER, Roger vii
SISLER, George Herald 130 131 Cassius 132 Mary 132
SISLER, Herman 128
SITTS, Phil vii
SLAYMAN, Joe vii Ruby vii
SOMERVILLE, Chas. 118 Emily Howard 118 Lina M 118
SORRICK, M. C. 132
STAATS, Richard vii
STEADMAN, Dr. C. G. 109
SWAIN, Walter S. 120
THOMAS, Cappy 128
THORN, Kate 134
TRAUBEL, Horace 4
TURNER, Lil Joe 10
U. S. Inf. 18th Regt. 17 18
VORIS, Gen. A. C. 89
WADSWORTH, Wm. 116
WAGGONER, Dr. Jos. 118
WAITE, Chas. S. 31
WESTERN RESERVE COLLEGE, 17-21 27 42 57 85 123
WHITMAN, Walt 3 4
WILLIAMS, Ike ix 127-131 Jim 127 128 130
WITTER, Mary 109
ZANE, Chas. S. 5

ABOUT THE AUTHOR

RICHARD J. STAATS was born in Akron, Ohio in 1940. After graduating from Manchester High School, he went on to pursue both a Bachelors (1964) and Masters (1970) Degree in Education from the University of Akron. A retired public school teacher, Staats is also an avid Civil War historian, who has traveled extensively for his research. The focus of his research is primarily on the views and experiences of the people of Portage County, Ohio during the Civil War era.

Staats currently has five books available through Heritage Books. In the *Grassroots History of the American Civil War* are: *Volume I, The Life and Times of Private Ephraim Cooper, One of Mr. Lincoln's First Volunteers*; *Volume II, The Bully Seventh Ohio Volunteer Infantry*; *Volume III, Captain Cotter's Battery*; and *Volume IV, The Life and Times of Colonel William Stedman of the 6th Ohio Cavalry*. The last work is *A Grassroots History of Baseball, Days of the Rosewood Bat and the Silver Ball*.

Staats and his wife Lora reside in Portage County, Ohio.

00412 8149